Fea...
& Fasting

what works
what doesn't
and why

MW01257588

Feasting
& Fasting
what works
what doesn't
and why

Shane Idleman

Published by
El Paseo Publications

Feasting & Fasting:
What Works, What Doesn't, and Why

Copyright © 2018 Shane Idleman

All rights reserved. No part of this publication may be reproduced or distributed in any form or by any means or stored in a database or retrieval system without the prior written permission from the publisher and/or author.

Published by El Paseo Publications
shaneidleman.net

Printed in the United States of America

Scripture taken from the New King James Version®. Copyright © 1982 by Thomas Nelson. Used by permission. All rights reserved. Scriptures and quotes within quotation marks are exact quotes; whereas, paraphrased Scriptures and quotes are often italicized.

Scripture quotations marked (NIV) are taken from the Holy Bible, New International Version®, NIV®. Copyright © 1973, 1978, 1984, 2011 by Biblica, Inc.™ Used by permission of Zondervan. All rights reserved worldwide. www.zondervan.com The "NIV" and "New International Version" are trademarks registered in the United States Patent and Trademark Office by Biblica, Inc.™

Scripture quotations marked (NASB) taken from the New American Standard Bible® (NASB), Copyright © 1960, 1962, 1963, 1968, 1971, 1972, 1973, 1975, 1977, 1995 by The Lockman Foundation. Used by permission. www.Lockman.org.

ISBN-13: 978-1718606234

ISBN-10: 1718606230

Acknowledgments

A special thanks to Liz Smith at Reformed Editorial Services and Christine Ramsey and Shawn Gosik for their insight, changes, and suggestions. Thanks also go to Diane Idleman for editing it many times over and to Jusika Martinez for cover design. Special thanks to Susie Woodruff at Westside Christian Fellowship, whose assistance in multiple areas allowed me to finish this project. And finally, I am grateful to my loving wife and my four wonderful children. I thank God that they have a passion for health as well.

Contents

A Must-Read Introduction: The Miracle of Fasting

When the body rests and is allowed to heal, many call the results *miraculous*, but this is just how God created us. Fasting not only creates an environment of health and healing, but more importantly, it facilitates spiritual growth. Obviously, God can choose to heal miraculously, but He also allows the body to heal and rejuvenate itself. I'm not promoting a fountain of youth—our DNA self-destructs as we age. Unfortunately, most people help that process along by not caring for the priceless, wonderful gift that God has given them. We teach stewarding our finances, our marriages, and our giftings in our churches, but why not our health? Granted, the physical benefits of fasting are secondary—the spiritual benefits are the priority.

This journey is not only about *physical* weight and health but *spiritual* weight and health as well. We are encouraged throughout the New Testament "not [to] labor for the food which perishes, but for the food which endures to everlasting life" (John 6:27). Our focus should be on spiritual things—that is, seek God first, and everything else will be added. Make Him the priority, not health and fitness.

Answering the questions presented in the subtitle, "What Works, What Doesn't, and Why," is actually very simple. What works? God's design and biblical principles. What doesn't work? Neither fitness obsession nor neglect—both are harmful. Why should we look to God's principles? They are guardrails through the canyons of life. They don't prevent us from enjoying life; they protect us from falling.

This is not an exhaustive study on fasting or nutrition but a resource to fan the flames in that direction. The recommended resources and sermon links located at the end may help answer additional questions. The sections entitled "My Fasting Experience"; "What Does the Bible Say about Food?"; and "What Did My Blood Say about Healthy Choices?" may also help to answer questions and provide motivation and encouragement for the beginner as well as the experienced faster—from preparing to cleansing to stabilizing weight. For this reason, resist the tendency to skip ahead, since each chapter builds to the conclusion. In 2015, I was forty-five pounds heavier than I am now. It took time, patience, and perseverance. Don't give up—look up!

This book was written based on personal experience and observation as well as many outside reputable resources. *If professional assistance is needed, the services of a capable authority are recommended.* **The views expressed in this book should not replace professional medical advice.** Readers should seek medical supervision before starting or altering a dietary plan, including fasting.

Although I recommend many articles and authors, I do not endorse them or always agree with their position. My goal is to offer the reader as much information as possible while keeping the book as short as possible. Links are provided for e-book users. Simply click the link that you are interested in (you must be online for this feature to work). If you're reading the printed version of this book, my encouragement is to also download the e-book version so that you can read the articles and listen to the sermons that are mentioned throughout this book.

At the time of this writing, I'm hoping to offer the e-book as a free resource to simply help people, for "freely you have received; freely give" (Matt. 10:8).

Website links are current up to the printing date. Neither the publisher nor the author assumes responsibility for errors or changes that occur after publication.

PART ONE
The Spiritual Benefits of Fasting

The Pain of Discipline over the Pain of Regret

You choose: Will it be the pain of discipline or the pain of regret? One yields a sense of extreme fulfillment; the other, a lingering sense of defeat. Ironically, we pray for God to heal when we should also pray for the self-discipline to change harmful habits. Fasting is hard because self-denial is hard (discipline), and overindulging is not rewarding (regret). It becomes a never-ending cycle of defeat unless we break the cycle by choosing discipline over regret as we seek the will of God.

God teaches us through discipline because He loves us. We are also encouraged to discipline our bodies. We cannot effectively be filled with the Spirit and lack discipline. Our faith is not passive; it's active faith. Romans 6:16 (NASB) sheds much-needed light: "Do you not know that when you present yourselves to someone as slaves for obedience, you are slaves of the one whom you obey, either of sin resulting in death, or of obedience resulting in righteousness?" Either way, we are slaves—we are either God's servant or a slave to our passions and desires. Self-discipline is a fruit of the Spirit, according to 2 Timothy 1:7. Those who say that discipline is legalism are dead wrong. **We are called to yield to the Spirit** and quench sin—but when we yield to sin, we quench the Spirit. Fleshly appetites are subdued when fasting. Fasting is challenging because the flesh always wants to negotiate with us. It says, "Can't we meet in the middle? Don't completely remove food—that's too extreme!"

Self-control is also required for leadership. In Titus 1:8 (NIV), Paul adds that a leader "must be hospitable, one who loves what is good, who is self-controlled, upright, holy and disciplined." John Wesley required fasting so that his leaders disciplined their appetites rather than allowed their appetites to rule them. It's been said for centuries that no man who cannot command himself is fit to command another. Paul told the Corinthians that he strikes a blow to his body and makes it his slave so that he will not be disqualified for service (1 Cor. 9:27). An *undisciplined leader* is an oxymoron.

We also see the power of fasting in Joel 1:14: "Consecrate a fast, call a sacred assembly; gather the elders and all the inhabitants of the land into the house of the Lord your God, and cry out to the Lord." The magnitude of the situation determined the response. God's people had departed from Him. The call was to return through fasting, prayer, and broken-ness. Fasting is depriving the flesh of its appetite as we pray and seek God's will and mercy. We are saying, "The flesh got me into this predicament, now it's time to seek God's mercy and humble myself before Him."

Obviously, people have overcome challenges without fasting, but fasting adds extra strength, especially when overcoming addictions. One addiction may end, but others can continue. The alcoholic switches to caffeine, the nicotine addict switches to sugar, and the opioid user switches to food. It's a never-ending cycle, but fasting can break the cycle. However, fasting is not a cure-all or a magic wand; it's a spiritual discipline designed to aid in victory. Again, choose the pain of discipline over the pain of regret.

Fasting—The Physical Affects the Spiritual

Through fasting, our body becomes a servant instead of a master. When Jesus directs us, the outcome is always beneficial, spiritually *and* physically. Notice He said, "When you fast" (Matt. 6:16). Scripture doesn't say, "When you sin, and if you fast," but rather, "If you sin" and "When you fast." The obvious goal and benefit of fasting is spiritual, but there are physical benefits as well. **Can we pray and seek God with all our heart with a headache, tight pants, and a sluggish, lethargic body strung out on our favorite addictive substance?** Of course not. Does the way you feel affect your productivity and the quality of your life? Absolutely. Our diet affects key hormones such as serotonin for relaxation, dopamine for pleasure, glutamate for healthy thinking, and noradrenaline for handling stress. If we allow junk food and addictions to control our attitude and productivity, it will hinder what we do for God. When we're always dealing with stress, anxiety, and sickness, can we do much for God? No, we will be limited. Granted, there are those who, through no fault of their own, have a debilitating illness. I'm assuming the reader understands that I'm talking to those who *can* make changes.

What you put in the mouth (body) and the mind (soul) affects the spirit—and when you feed the spirit, it affects the body and the soul. I'm often asked to pray for panic attacks, angry outbursts, and anxiety. That can be done, and God honors prayer, but are we opening the door to these things by not halting highly addictive caffeine, sugar, opioid, or nicotine habits? Or are we renewing our mind by meditating on the Word and spending time in prayer? The physical affects the spiritual, and the spiritual affects the physical. Much of the healing that I have witnessed over the years was the result of renewed stewardship of the body.

We also know that many emotions such as anger, bitterness, and jealousy are toxic to the body. Health also involves healthy emotions. Having a forgiving, loving, joy-filled heart does wonders for the body. Serotonin, for example, is increased when the heart is right. This crucial chemical (also affected by diet and exercise) impacts our mood at a very deep level and contributes to an overall state of well-being.

Again, I'm not suggesting that health should *replace* God and prayer but that it should *complement* them—that we steward the gift of health. No one is perfect, but we are called to discipline our bodies and use wisdom. God does heal miraculously, even in our ignorance, but that shouldn't cause us to neglect our health.

With more than 12 million US children being obese, and millions more being malnourished, the need to address this topic has never been greater. Caffeine, soft drinks, and junk food are fueling the disease epidemic. **Yet we pray for God to heal rather than ask for His help with the self-**

discipline to change harmful habits. What's wrong with this picture? *"There are multitudes of diseases which have their origin in fullness, and might have their end in fasting."*[1]

The myth that fasting is bad for you is unfounded and has been disproved numerous times. Be careful when getting counsel from those who profit from that advice or from those who know little about how the body heals itself. I vividly recall the story of a man who had colon surgery yet may not have needed it had he just changed his diet. The hospital even fed him a greasy sloppy joe after he awoke from surgery. A lack of wisdom has been our downfall. (For more about how the physical affects the spiritual, search for "The Doctrine of Man (Sin & the Curse)" at WCFAV.org.)

It's been estimated that nearly 75 percent of US clinical trials in medicine are paid for by private companies who benefit. For example, "Statins are good for you"—paid for by pharmaceutical companies that make them.[2] Or "Take this drug to feel better"—never mind the fact that side effects include internal bleeding, seizures, and panic attacks. Or "Eat this children's cereal"—just ignore the harmful GMOs, food coloring, additives, preservatives, and toxins. America, wake up! You are what you eat. **Fasting doesn't kill us; overconsumption and consuming empty food does.** *Companies are often driven by revenue, but no one profits from fasting except the faster.* Processed food is cheap and convenient. It often contains stimulating and addictive ingredients and flavor-enhancing chemicals. When was the last time you saw an advertisement for broccoli, blueberries, or kale?

Disease is often a problem of toxicity created by what we consume, ingest, or breathe—and fasting is the detox solution. Granted, spiritual health and wholeness are the goals when fasting, but the physical benefits

---

[1] James Morrison, quoted in Arthur Wallis, *God's Chosen Fast* (Fort Washington, PA: Christian Literature Crusade, 1977), 104–105 (emphasis added).

[2] See "New Cholesterol Guidelines May Put 13 Million More on Statin Drugs" at Mercola.com, https://articles.mercola.com/sites/articles/archive/2014/04/02/cho lesterol-statin-drugs-guidelines.aspx.

are worthwhile. Dr. J. H. Tilden said, "After fifty-five years of sojourning in the wilderness of medical therapeutics, I am forced to declare ... that fasting is the only reliable, specific, therapeutic eliminant known to man."[3]

Dr. Joel Fuhrman noted, "The body's wondrous ability to [self-digest] and destroy needless tissue such as fat, tumors, blood vessel plaque, and other nonessential and diseased tissues, while conserving essential tissues, gives the fast the ability to restore ... youth to the system."[4] Most research on cancer and fasting supports the healing process as well. For example, the goal of chemotherapy is to stop or slow the growth of cancer cells, but it's been said that the body has a natural, God-given way to do this without harming the healthy cells—*fasting*. Fasting is not a panacea; it simply provides an environment for healing.

Dr. Yuri Nikolayev, a psychiatrist at the University of Moscow, treated schizophrenics with water fasts for 25 to 30 days. This was followed by eating healthy foods for 30 days. About 70 percent of his patients remained free from symptoms for the duration of the 6-year study. The health benefits of fasting are incredible.[5]

Did you know that Type 2 diabetes is nearly eliminated with proper diet when you stop fueling the disease and fast? It doesn't have to be a progressive disease. There is hope if you starve the fuel source and incorporate fasting. The reason you may find it nearly impossible to fast is because you might be withdrawing from poisons and addictive substances. Therefore, begin by eliminating junk food and educate yourself by reading the recommended resources. *Seek medical support and consultation if need be, but keep in mind that most are not supportive of fasting simply because they are trained to ease the pain rather than eliminate the problem.*

---

[3] Dr. J. H. Tilden, quoted in Herbert M. Shelton, *Fasting Can Save Your Life* (Tampa: Natural Hygiene Press, 1981), 36. Although I don't agree with all of Dr. Tilden's views, statements like this are very common in his books and articles regarding preventative healthcare.

[4] Joel Fuhrman, *Fasting and Eating for Health: A Medical Doctor's Program for Conquering Disease* (New York: St. Martin's Griffin, 1995).

[5] Dr. Yuri Nikolayev's research was conducted as the director of the fasting treatment unit of Moscow Psychiatric Institute.

Drugs don't often cure the underlying problem, and they are toxic. Granted, there may be a time for certain medications, but they should be the last resort, not the first. For example, antibiotics wipe out harmful bacteria as well as good bacteria, and some antibiotics can even be harmful. For instance, check out the side effects on WebMD for Ciprofloxacin (Cipro).[6] It even has black box warnings, the strictest labeling requirements the FDA can mandate for prescription drugs. Not only is it prescribed, it's overprescribed and given to kids and the elderly. Yes, all antibiotics have side effects, but doesn't that tell us something?[7] If the underlying problem of poor health isn't dealt with, illness will return with vengeance. **This is why many are chronically sick—they are always medicating and never healing.**

At this point, questions often arise about vaccines. Do your own research. Read what the CDC says about results as well as the toxicity levels of vaccines. Some of the ingredients such as aluminum, mercury, and formaldehyde—not to mention other toxic ingredients—are neurotoxins that harm the brain. Those who say we shouldn't worry about ingredients because an apple also contains formaldehyde truly have not done their homework. Is it wise to inject a virus directly into the bloodstream? Is vaccination about helping people or generating income? You be the judge.

For those desiring more information, read pro-vaccine literature and books showing the other side, such as *The Sanctity of Human Blood*, then come to your own conclusion.[8] One thing is certain though: Children are

---

[6] See https://www.webmd.com/drugs/2/drug-1124-93/cipro-oral/ciprofloxacin-oral/details.

[7] The US National Library of Medicine National Institutes of Health released an article outlining some of the side effects here: https://www.ncbi.nlm.nih.gov/pmc/articles/PMC3421593, or search online for "Adverse Effects of Antimicrobials via Predictable or Idiosyncratic Inhibition of Host Mitochondrial Components."

[8] *The Sanctity of Human Blood: Vaccination Is Not Immunization* by Tim O'Shea is a book that many recommend. It is not written from a Christian perspective but from a medical perspective. I don't agree with all his conclusions, nor am I fully endorsing it, but it will provide research and solid facts for those desiring more information about vaccines.

receiving far too many shots. If the immune system is already taxed because of poor health and bad eating habits (e.g., sugar, food coloring, additives, and chemicals), injecting harmful bacteria into the system could escalate problems.

Fasting also lowers blood pressure and impacts blood sugar levels. If you're taking medication for either, you may find yourself overmedicating because the fast is working in conjunction with the medication, albeit naturally. *Medicine often takes the credit when it was God's design that did the healing.*

Again, fasting does not heal the body; it gives the body the optimal environment for healing. Fasting is a process that God created. Additionally, God-given food promotes life; man-created food does not. A recent example of this involved my youngest daughter. She was not breathing well at night. The physician said that her tonsils and adenoids were inflamed and needed to be removed. Knowing that tonsils and adenoids help with immunity, we tried a different route first. We completely changed her diet by removing all sugar (except light fruit and minimal dark honey). We focused on life-giving food and a daily nap. She was breathing well within a week, and an ear infection that had been lingering healed as well. The right nutrition, along with deep sleep, creates a powerful environment for healing. Are you receiving both?

A few months later, another daughter was advised to take amoxicillin for a tooth infection. The dentist said he would remove the tooth and install a metal brace for her to wear for a year. A quick diet change also resulted in her body healing itself, eliminating the need for any dental intervention. **Again, there may be a time for medication, but it should be the last resort, not the first.**

I have friends who are doctors, and I deeply respect them. They are highly trained in easing symptoms. *But most in the healthcare industry are not educated in fixing the cause.* For example, many men are told to take AndroGel because of low testosterone levels, but they can often increase their testosterone naturally by avoiding alcohol, exercising, eating healthy food, eliminating sugar, lowering stress, fasting, and taking vitamin D. I knew a man whose testosterone level went from 225 to 530 within eight months by changing his lifestyle. The side effects of testosterone therapy should be motivation enough to make changes.

A few years ago, a doctor wanted to send me home with two different high blood pressure medications. Before leaving, I asked him if he used the large cuff for men when he took my blood pressure. He didn't. When he did, the blood pressure reading came in normal. I can list many more examples of inconsistency, such as a sign in a doctor's office that said in big letters right above the coffee pot: "DON'T CONSUME BEFORE A STRESS TEST." Let's wake up! Our health is on the line.

We need more physicians who understand how the body works and can help the patient from the inside out. They need us, and we need them. But I cringe at the number of Type 2 diabetes patients who are sent home from their doctor's office with even more medication or the countless overweight individuals who leave with high blood pressure drugs instead of real solutions that work. Sadly, we often prefer the "quick fix" approach. But please don't misunderstand—I'm not suggesting that we bypass prayer, nor am I insinuating that we disregard the advice of physicians or that we don't need medication. We must use wisdom. Again, I have seen God heal primarily through fixing the toxic state of the body. How can we pray, "Lord, please heal my heart disease," while driving to McDonald's?

Fasting Applies Extra Pressure to the Spiritual Realm

In Matthew 17:21, Jesus said that a certain evil spirit does not go out of a person except by prayer and fasting. Some manuscripts disagree on whether this verse should be included or not, but the principle is found throughout Scripture: *Fasting applies pressure to the spiritual realm.* Arthur Wallis notes, **"Often, pressure has to be maintained before there is a breakthrough in heavenly warfare."**[9] It appears that some demonic activity is not released until pressure is applied through prayer and fasting.

The weapons we use to fight Satan are not physical; they are spiritual. The weapons should match the warfare! Satan cannot be eliminated with an AR-15, but we *can* fast and pray. Those two high-caliber spiritual bullets do substantial damage. Open the Word, pray, meditate, and worship for the fatal blow: "'Not by might nor by power, but by My Spirit,' says the Lord of hosts" (Zech. 4:6).

---

[9] Wallis, *God's Chosen Fast*, 53 (emphasis added).

Two wills cannot successfully live in the same body—our self-will and God's will. We can't defeat what we feed. God's Word states, "For all that is in the world—the lust of the flesh, the lust of the eyes, and the pride of life—is not of the Father but is of the world" (1 John 2:16). Society says, "Be yourself! Embrace your longings! Feed your desires!" However, we know that gluttony and indulging the flesh never lead to spiritual victory, or any victory for that matter. Some strongholds hang on piece by piece. We must "resist the devil" and he will eventually flee (James 4:7). *Fasting disciplines the body, prayer and worship bind the enemy, and the Word provides wisdom.* Fasting ignites a hunger for God and provides direction. For example, I was energized to write this book during a long fast.

Don't misconstrue—I'm not promoting a works-based religion. I'm demonstrating the importance of spiritual disciplines that produce godly fruit. What is dead in your life that you know God is wanting to resurrect? What dream, goal, or godly ambition is waiting to be realized? Is there a stronghold that has been gripping your life? Do you desire a deeper walk with God and increased spiritual hunger? Do you need help in self-discipline and temperance? Do you need a breakthrough, direction, or peace? Is all hell breaking loose in your life? Are there great obstacles ahead? Then it's time to prepare for battle through prayer and fasting.

Ask God for direction and set a target date. Remove the hindrances within your home such as junk food and junk media—out of sight, out of mind. Fuel the completion of your fast by praying, reading, worshiping, and listening to sermons on fasting. Have a prayer list available. **It's a battle—a hunger strike against hell. It's challenging and difficult, but the pain of discipline far outweighs the pain of regret.**

After I stumbled through my first seven-day water fast, Fox News contacted me to fly to New York to debate a pastor with opposing views on morality. My wife and I also met two Christian men who have encouraged me though their ministries—Jim Cymbala, pastor of the Brooklyn Tabernacle, and actor, producer, and evangelist Kirk Cameron. Additionally, God grew our church, expanded its reach, and healed old wounds. A perfect fast didn't do this, but God, through His mercy, honored my feeble attempt, and He will do the same for you.

The vast majority of the heroes of the faith fasted, and it's still very common in many places. But in America, our fullness is our downfall.

Leonard Ravenhill once said, "When there's something in the Bible that churches don't like [such as fasting], they call it legalism."[10]

Whether it's on the radio, television, the internet, or at church, we often hear that God has a wonderful plan for our life and that Christianity is easy and carefree. We have changed following Christ into an easy path rather than a narrow road. We've made Jesus a butler rather than a King. We want the cross light, the road easy, and the burdens lifted.

Spiritual disciplines are intended to not only break down strongholds but also to build us up. Yes, God blesses His people—we should pray for, enjoy, and encourage His blessings. But a wonderful, comfortable life is not always a blessing. As the Bible teaches, the presence and the power of God in our lives is always a blessing: "The Lord gives strength to his people; the Lord blesses his people with peace" (Ps. 29:11 NIV).

A Christian is called to be a lean, fighting machine. I'm not talking about body weight but spiritual weight—weight to pull down strongholds. Leonard Ravenhill has said, "How can you pull down strongholds of Satan if you don't even have the strength to turn off your TV?" We could add "How can we pull down strongholds of Satan if we don't even have the strength to say no to food?"

I'm not teaching perfectionism. No one has complete mastery over the flesh, but our goal should be victory rather than constant defeat. Deeply embedded addictions can be reversed by starving the flesh. We are not powerless. We give control to either the flesh or the Spirit. James 4:5 reminds us that our spirit has "envious yearnings." Do we yield to these yearnings, or do we give in to the pull of the flesh? **We will crave more of what we feed. Fasting silences the voice of the flesh.**

We all fall short. The only difference between those who succeed and those who fail is that those who succeed get back up again. Fasting doesn't twist God's arm; it realigns our heart with His and gets us back on track; it gives us wisdom and discernment for crucial issues. Discernment is one of

---

[10] Commonly attributed to Leonard Ravenhill. He was known for many of these types of quotes in his sermons and books, such as *Why Revival Tarries* (Bloomington, MN: Bethany House Publishers, 2004).

our greatest challenges today. I came across this news clip some time ago that illustrates my point:

> A 17-year old Dutch girl who died on Monday during a bungee jump misheard instructions and jumped on the "no jump" instruction. One of the Spanish instructors on the bridge when the teenager plunged 40 meters to her death told the police that the girl jumped before her harness was clipped on to the bungee cord. An instructor told Spanish television channel RTVE that she had said, "No jump. No jump," but that the girl may have misheard and thought she said, "Now jump."

So tragic. Too many today are listening to the wrong voice. Are you? The goal of sin is to destroy our testimony and our lives by following the wrong voice. Obviously, we are to spend time in God's Word seeking wisdom and discernment, but fasting aids the process. **We don't want to go when God says, "No!"**

Fasting–The Secret to Spiritual Power

Matthew 26:41 reminds us to watch and pray so that we will not fall into temptation. Jesus said that the spirit is willing, but the flesh is weak. Fasting strengthens the spirit and sharpens the sword.

A story I've heard numerous times brings this point home. Two lumberjacks decided to compete to see who could cut down the most trees. As the clock wound down, the younger man noticed that the old lumberjack kept taking breaks. He thought, "Surely I will win—this man is lazy and weak." But when the day was over, the old lumberjack had chopped down more trees. Perplexed, the young man asked, "How did you do that?" The older man replied, "Son, what you mistook for unnecessary breaks were necessary. I sharpened my ax each time."

Fasting sharpens spiritual insight, wisdom, and discernment. You're either controlling your body or your body is controlling you. We drive a certain way to pick up our addiction, we go to certain places because of our addiction, and we schedule things around our addiction. *Do we realize just how much our addictions control us versus our controlling them?*

On another note, imagine heading to lunch in a crowded mall. You and your family are famished from running errands. Just before leaving, you notice that your three-year-old is no longer with you—panic sets in! You must find your child at any cost. Are you going to eat first? Of course not. The passion to find your child is far greater than the desire to eat. **That's exactly what fasting is—the desire to seek God is greater than the desire to eat.**

Some may argue, "Fasting is too extreme!" Are we not living in extremely difficult times? As the saying goes, desperate times call for desperate measures. Dr. Caldwell Esselstyn reminds us about the other side of the coin: "Half a million people a year will have their chests opened up and a vein taken from their leg and sewn onto their coronary artery."[11] He calls that extreme, and so do I. We reap what we sow.

Recent statistics reveal that the opioid crisis is killing tens of thousands of people and that alcoholism continues to ravish homes. Millions are walking away from their faith each year, marriages are in shambles, families are deteriorating, and suicide is an epidemic. I call that extreme! It's time that Christians get extreme in their warfare if they truly desire victory. A strong attack by the enemy requires a strong defense. When God moves, prayer and fasting have often been the catalyst.

Prepare yourself by getting your body and mind ready. If possible, wean off everything that is hurting your health, both spiritual and physical. Most choices lead either to the filling of the Spirit or to quenching and grieving Him. Giving in to one area of weakness lowers our defense in other areas. This aligns with 1 Peter 2:11, in which Peter urges his readers "to abstain from fleshly lusts which wage war against the soul."

Prayer, fasting, the Word, and worship starve the enemy's influence. As the flesh submits, we become more in tune with the things of God. A stagnant spiritual life turns into flowing waters. The mind becomes uncluttered and focused. The things of God, rather than the things of the world, begin to dominate our thinking.

Why wait? Procrastination keeps the car in neutral. You can't steer what's not moving; start the process of change today. An incident from the American Revolution illustrates the power of procrastination. It is reported

---

[11] *Forks Over Knives*, directed by Lee Fulkerson (Monica Beach Media, 2011).

that Colonel Rall, commander of the British troops in New Jersey, was playing cards when a courier brought an urgent message stating that General George Washington was crossing the Delaware River. Rall put the letter in his pocket and didn't bother to read it until the game was finished, but it was too late. His procrastination cost him his victory and his life.

Begin today. You've probably fallen so many times that you have lost count—so have I. Don't focus on past mistakes. As a famous poem declares:

> For all of life is like [a] race,
> with ups and downs and all,
> and all you have to do to win
> is rise each time you fall.[12]

God honors perseverance, not perfection.

---

[12] Commonly attributed to Dr. D. H. "Dee" Groberg. If you need encouragement, find the poem online entitled "The Race." It's well worth the read.

PART TWO
Fasting—When, Why, and How

Common Questions about Fasting

If I've learned one thing pastoring, it is this: When you allow the Holy Spirit to take control of your physical appetite, your spiritual appetite for God increases. Through strength in Christ, not willpower, we find victory. And nothing feels better than victory over the flesh. This is age-old wisdom: "Fasting begets prophets and strengthens strong men. Fasting makes lawgivers wise; it is the soul's safeguard, the body's trusted comrade, the armor of the champion, the training of the athlete."[13]

Fasting does not motivate God to love me more, but I find that I love *Him* more. Fasting prepares the heart. God "acts on behalf of those who wait for him" (Isa. 64:4 NIV). Do you need God to act? Wait on Him through prayer and fasting.

---

[13] Commonly attributed to Basil, bishop of Caesarea in the fourth century, and an early church father. History reveals that he fasted often.

What is fasting?

There are a lot of creative ideas, but the definition of biblical fasting is to abstain from any regular source of strength and nourishment, food and liquid. Daniel was the exception. He avoided all appealing food. One reason the Daniel approach was and still is so powerful is because the body consumes only God-given food. Junk food has zero life-giving benefits. I call it the *Daniel Healthy Eating Plan* instead of a fast.

As appetite decreases, prayer must increase. Fasting without prayer is simply a diet without spiritual benefits. My encouragement is that fasting becomes a lifestyle. Herbert M. Shelton offers a good reminder: "When a man learns his limitations in food consumption, and respects these, he will remain well. . . . A return to coffee and tobacco, to alcohol and poisoned soft drinks, to overwork and late hours, to unventilated bedrooms and slothfulness, to overeating and the conventional diet" will cause disease to return.[14] Fasting must complement a healthy diet, not take the place of it.

I often wonder how many diseases could be prevented and/or reversed by fasting and eating clean. Multiple sclerosis, for example, is a disease where the immune system slowly consumes the protective sheath that covers the nerves. Can this happen because the body is kept in a toxic state and not allowed to heal? Parkinson's, another problematic disease, is primarily caused by low dopamine levels. In many cases, dopamine-generating cells have died; even experts do not know why these cells die. Could they have been restored, or new ones created, if the body was allowed time to detox and consume life-giving food? Alzheimer's, another deteriorating disease, is caused when brain cells slowly die and healthy ones are not replicated. As a result, brain tissue has fewer and fewer nerve cells and connections. This leads to the mental and physical symptoms that we see in those who suffer with it. Could fasting, while consuming life-building food at other times, reverse or prevent some of these illnesses? Fasting allows the body to heal, and life-giving food provides many healing properties designed to bring restoration and health to the body.

---

[14] Herbert M. Shelton, *Fasting Can Save Your Life* (Tampa: Natural Hygiene Press, 1981), 67.

Many say, "What's the use? I'm getting old; failing health is normal." Don't buy into that. Aging should be all the more reason to apply what we've been discussing. Whether it's a 100-year-old man who mows lawns or the 100-year-old farmer who still works the field (albeit much more slowly), healthy living leads to success most of the time. We should take care of the gift that God has given us. Moses still had his eyesight and his strength at 120 years of age (Deut. 34:7).

Consider intermittent fasting as a way to get started. Our ancestors may have eaten this way when food was scarce. Intermittent fasting focuses on short-term fasts. The goal is to keep the body in a ketogenic (fat-burning) state by consuming certain low-carb foods. It's a good place to start, but water fasts are much more beneficial for detox and cleansing. (More on intermittent fasting later.)

Where do I start?

Don't focus on length just yet. Simply step out in faith. Begin with a meal or two, educate yourself, and seek medical advice if needed. You may want to tell your physician what you're doing and ask if he or she can review blood work and monitor vitals. It can be motivating to see the benefits of fasting in a before-and-after blood panel. Pray and ask God for direction and encouragement. I have included helpful sermons and resources at the end of this book; it was actually a sermon I heard six days into a fast that kept me from quitting.

If you truly start feeling sick and can tell something is off (as opposed to feeling tired, grumpy, lightheaded, dizzy, or hungry), that may be a good indication to drink some juice or eat a light meal. Then get back on track. While fasting, there are boosts of energy followed by big letdowns, although becoming sick can be something different. Many have fought through these feelings, but it's an area where wisdom is needed.

The body often retraces past problems in order to heal them. If you had a cold some time back, for example, you might see those same symptoms again while the body is healing. Experts are divided on whether you should push through feeling sick and flu-like or take a small amount of food. In my case, I press through as long as it is not intense and if my scheduled commitments allow for it. Self-control and willpower are two key components of fasting. *There's no way around it—the power of the made-up mind tilts the scale in your favor.*

For many years, I thought I was hypoglycemic, so I had a good excuse not to fast. I learned later that I was just addicted to sugar. Be patient; health is a lifestyle, not a short-term fix. Fasting success is largely a mental state. Your body has been conditioned to eat at certain intervals, not to mention having addictions that want to be fed often.

Why should I fast? How is starving beneficial?

Fasting starves the flesh—the fuel source of sin. Fasting also provides fertile soil for the fruit of the Spirit, such as self-discipline. The lust of the flesh sidetracks us whenever it can—the more we feed it, the more we fuel it. Fasting starves the flesh so we can be filled with the Spirit. Drudgery becomes delight.

Fasting is not starving in a physical sense; it's the removal of food for a season. The body switches from burning glucose as fuel to burning ketones when fat is broken down and converted to energy—just like God designed us.

We are designed to fast for spiritual, physical, and emotional benefit. Mental clarity and brain function are heightened as well. Instead of dying, we are repairing. Rarely does anyone in America die of fasting, but millions die because of overeating. *Fasting is not the problem; feasting is.*

How long should I fast?

There is no quick answer, so research is important. If we are talking about fasting for health reasons, ideally one should fast for as long as it takes to heal or detox. The goal determines the length. The longer the better in most cases. I don't want to shock anyone, but water fasts of three or four weeks are not uncommon. Most who have fasted this long prepared themselves beforehand or attended a fasting retreat center with medical supervision.

Don't forget to factor in the re-feeding phase. After an extended fast, the stomach shuts down, and care should be taken when reintroducing food. For example, those who fast for one week should allow a few extra days for light fruit. As fasting time increases, the length of the re-feeding phase should increase as well. If fasting for spiritual reasons, pray, set a time frame, and fulfill it. For me, the spiritual benefit is the primary goal; the health benefits are secondary. I would encourage most people to incorporate a one-day fast of water into their weekly schedule. The health benefits are incredible as long as the person maintains a good diet.

How do I get back on track if I fall?

Most people do not fast perfectly when beginning. On my first seven-day water fast, I used bone broth, a few scoops of protein powder, and a handful of nuts to get through. I'm not suggesting that you cave in; I am offering hope if you misstep.

During my first full-day water fast years ago, I had a cup of orange juice to get me through. God doesn't look at caloric intake; He looks at the condition of your heart. However, to receive the full benefits of fasting, it's best to refrain from any food or juice, if possible, and drink water only.

If you fall, get back on track and move forward. Isn't that the Christian walk? The key to long-term change is a lifestyle change. Today's choices affect tomorrow's reward. It's important to take care of your body before and after fasting. Again, fasting doesn't replace a healthy lifestyle; it complements it.

Even so, if you are fasting for physical health, what is the benefit of going weeks without coffee, junk food, nicotine, and so on, then fall right back into harmful habits once the fast is over? Your goal should be the opposite—to keep fueling a healthy lifestyle. It's been estimated that every pound of fat requires an extra mile or two of blood vessels. That means more work for the body, especially the heart. Two and a half years ago, I was carrying approximately 45 extra miles of blood vessels. Amazing!

It took me a few years to finally work up the courage to do a seven-day water fast. Don't take on too much. Start with small steps. The body eventually adapts. Now I can go a full day with little difficulty. The fact that you are stepping out in faith pleases God. If you fall, get back up and move forward. *Direction, not perfection, takes you to the finish line.*

Don't allow fasting, or any spiritual discipline, to become rigid and mechanical or a system of works. Type A people need to avoid rules and regulations and striving for perfection, whereas passive people may need to be aggressive with a plan and a purpose. Don't beat yourself up if you slip. Get back up! Some of my fasts have not been completed perfectly. I must have said no a thousand times, and I almost allowed a half-dozen failures to stop me from finishing.

I can't explain why, but looking back, I think God uses failures to demonstrate His grace and mercy. Obviously, staying on track is ideal, but sometimes we fall. Like children, we are growing in our walk with the Lord. Infants learning to walk don't quit when they fall—they get back up. *Eventually, you will walk where you once fell.*

Can I drink coffee, tea, or soft drinks when fasting?

The short answer is no. Some say it's okay to drink coffee on a fast, but in my opinion, this is bad advice, probably given by someone who enjoys this addictive substance. Not only are you continually re-introducing many harmful chemicals into the system that your body is trying to eliminate, but you are also keeping the addiction alive. The chemical acrylamide in roasted coffee beans has been shown to increase cancer risk in lab animals.[15] We may someday see warning labels on roasted coffee for this very reason.

Water is crucial to health, but stimulants like caffeine act as a diuretic and push water out of the body. And from removing toxins to hydrating every cell, water is a vital resource, especially when fasting. All the ways that the body removes toxins are affected by water. From mucus to urine—pure, clean water cleanses the entire system. Sipping it throughout the day is ideal since too much at one time can affect certain balances (e.g., drinking more than a few cups at a time). I'm not a fan of distilled, dead water or alkaline water (e.g., a pH greater than seven). I aim for clean spring water when possible.

When you don't have enough water, your body will take it from other places such as your skin and joints. This affects everything from mobility to aging. Hydration is key. It should also come from foods with a high water content such as papayas, watermelons, oranges, and many vegetables. *Remember, food either gives life or feeds disease.*

---

[15] "Acrylamide and Cancer Risk," National Cancer Institute, https://www.cancer.gov/about-cancer/causes-prevention/risk/diet/acrylamide-fact-sheet.

I always excused my poor attitude with statements such as, "I had a bad day," "I'm under a lot of stress," or "I'm tired." Ironically, I was the primary cause of my bad days, stress, and fatigue. Addiction to caffeine, for example, can fuel anger. The *Diagnostic and Statistical Manual for Mental Disorders* lists caffeine-related disorders such as caffeine intoxication, caffeine-induced anxiety disorder, and caffeine-induced sleep disorder—all of which can lead to angry outbursts, severe anxiety, and extreme irritability.[16] *If we believe that we can drink a high-powered stimulant day in and day out and not have it affect health, we are gravely mistaken.*

As a person who once loved a few strong cups of coffee and who still struggles from time to time, I understand that moderation is the key. But can an addictive substance ever be consumed in moderation? Maybe, but just ask an alcoholic why they can't have just one drink.

Caffeine intake in the form of energy drinks, soda, tea, and coffee is highly addictive and damages health. This may be one reason why we are seeing a rise in anger via road rage. Caffeine keeps the body in a constant state of stress, resulting in adrenal fatigue. There is little wonder why the body breaks down often and never overcomes fatigue. If your eyesight is failing, try removing coffee and sugar from your diet. This simple change did wonders for me.

Contrary to popular belief, stimulants don't help fatigue; they contribute to it by robbing Peter to pay Paul. The short-term results do not outweigh the long-term damage. Granted, we won't be fully free of anger and anxiety. We live in a sinful world that often results in sinful attitudes. However, don't throw the baby out with the bathwater and dismiss caffeine as a catalyst for anger and anxiety. Most people that I've counseled who have damaged their family through anger are often addicted to caffeine, nicotine, alcohol, drugs, or other substances. **Clearly, health plays a vital role in our overall attitude. When we feed the body and spirit what they need, everything works better.**

---

[16] *Diagnostic and Statistical Manual of Mental Disorders*, 5th ed. (Arlington, VA: American Psychiatric Association, 2013). More can be found at the US National Library of Medicine National Institutes of Health: https://www.ncbi. nlm.nih.gov/pmc/articles/PMC3777290.

We were created to consume living, life-sustaining, God-given foods that nourish and support a healthy body, not dead, life-depleting food from a factory. The life of the food is to be deposited into the body to support and maintain life. If you can avoid unhealthy food, you'll be well on your way to better vitality.

I vividly remember a comment from a clinical nutritionist that motivated me: *"Discontinuing caffeine intake leads to significant improvements in health ... far more than just dieting alone."*[17] He also made the connection to depression, anxiety, and panic attacks from excessive caffeine.

Since caffeine runs along the same biochemical pathways in the brain as cocaine, opium, and amphetamines, quitting can be a nightmare. My suggestion is to back off day by day until intake is very minimal and use organic green tea (light caffeine) whenever possible. You'll be shocked by the results. Granted, the first week may be very difficult, but it will be worth it. The withdrawal symptoms alone reveal the power of this drug. I was fascinated to read that the logo of a very popular coffee franchise represents a seductive image that allures and entices. How ironic.

This begs the question as to how many are suffering mentally and physically simply because of poor choices—continuing the addiction rather than removing the cause of the problem. Not in all cases but in most, depression, anxiety, irritability, and the like could be severely curtailed if health (spiritual and physical) were a priority.

In the same way that a hiker feels released, energized, and unburdened after removing a heavy backpack, you'll feel released and energized after removing stimulants. I became a more patient, kinder, and more easygoing person when I quit abusing coffee. I never realized how much it was contributing to my mental state until at least a week after weaning off, and the withdrawals brought out the worst in me. As much as I wanted to be

---

[17] Stephen Cherniske, *Caffeine Blues: Wake Up to the Hidden Dangers of America's #1 Drug* (New York: Warner Books, 1998), 30. Although not written from a Christian perspective, I recommend this book for those desiring more information on this topic.

filled with the Spirit, I was feeding my body a substance that was counterproductive.

I'm amazed at how much damage the human body can endure. I'm aware that most reading this will continue the habit of using caffeine. If so, do yourself a favor and lower the amount considerably. At a mini-mum, wean yourself off coffee, strong tea, soft drinks, nicotine, sugar, and processed food before fasting—it will help success.

What about health drinks and supplements?

Again, fasting is fasting from outside nourishment. Health drinks, such as Kombucha, can contain sugar as well as trace amounts of alcohol and caffeine. When I drank Kombucha I felt the small amount of alcohol; it became addictive and actually increased my craving for alcohol. If you have a history of alcohol addiction, avoid drinks with even minimal amounts.

Some recommend bone broth and various drinks to aid the body. Although they have some benefits, they can also reignite digestive juices, which lead to hunger. Having a cup of organic broth to take the edge off can occasionally help, but ideally, it's best to drink clean, pure water.

A big misconception about fasting is that you'll become sick because the body will lack vitamins and minerals. This is not so—the body pulls vitamins and minerals from stored areas when you are fasting. For those concerned about this, there are water beverages that contain just water, vitamins, minerals, and electrolytes.

The question also arises about noncaloric, naturally flavored carbonated water. Try to avoid these when possible. Not only could aluminum seep into the water, but we also don't know the purity of the water or the source of the so-called "natural" flavor. Having one might appease hunger, but I wouldn't get into the habit of having them often. It is the same with chewing gum or anything else that stimulates a taste reaction.

Supplementation

The topic of supplementation is very broad and too much to cover here but let me offer a suggestion. As a person who was once a big fan of supplementation, I have backed off considerably. I took it all: ginkgo biloba, elderberry, echinacea, and colloidal silver along with detox teas, green powders, vitamins, and essential oils. I stocked up on chlorophyll, calcium, and turmeric along with vitamin D, bee pollen, fish oil, and probiotics.

The bottom line is that nothing works better than fasting—nothing is even a close second. Many of these things can "supplement" our diet from time to time. For example, the Advanced Immunological Treatment and Research Medical Center in Mexico is combining vitamin C and K3 therapy to fight cancer.[18] But wisdom is needed since large quantities of supplements aren't always helpful. Just because something is natural doesn't always mean it is healthy when taken in abundance. For example, if you drop highly concentrated lemon drops (equivalent to 50 lemons) in water, is the body able to process that amount of overload? Look at how the body was designed by God.

Although some disagree, low doses of healthy herbs appear beneficial in killing toxins by inducing the body to increase detoxification enzymes. But again, too much can be harmful. I often avoid them when fasting (e.g., garlic, basil, turmeric, cinnamon, ginger, etc.). Even though I have cut way back, I do use light supplementation when needed such as turmeric, garlic, and vitamins that do not contain fillers or binders and that are not heat-treated.

No one has the market on truth in this area, and science is always learning, but one thing is certain: *The body was fearfully and masterfully made; allow it to heal itself by positioning everything in its favor, which may involve limiting supplementation if you are prone to go overboard.*

What about juicing?

Our body uses close to 50 percent of its energy to digest food. Fasting uses this vital energy to instead clean the body. Think of it this way: If a motor is only at half throttle, it will greatly impact performance. Juice fasting, though healthy, does not give the digestive system complete rest. However, the amount of energy used is relative to the type of food we

---

[18] See "The Cancer Killing Ratio . . . How 100:1 of Vitamin C and K3 Is Changing the Way We Fight Cancer!", CHIPSA, https://chipsahospital.org/1001 -the-cancer-killing-ratio-how-this-combination-of-vitamin-c-and-k3-is-chang ing-the-way-we-fight-cancer.

consume. For instance, a green juice drink is much easier to digest than steak and potatoes.

Juicing can be a good starting point with many benefits if vegetables are primarily used; fruit contains a great deal of sugar called *fructose*. Instead of calling it *fasting*, call it *juicing* or *juice cleansing* because that's what it is. Some recommend doing a juice cleanse every quarter in conjunction with or in addition to water fasting. Again, it does not take the place of water fasting, especially if the juice is not free of chemicals.

If we consume too much juice from fruit, we will ingest primarily sugar via fructose, minus the important cofactors such as fiber and enzymes that are absorbed when consuming the whole fruit. In my opinion, it's best to consume organic whole fruit instead of juicing it. Juice affects glucose and insulin levels in negative ways. Avoid store-bought juice because all the enzymes are destroyed in the pasteurization process, and you'll basically be drinking pure sugar. Juicing works well for people because they lose weight when calorie consumption is lowered, but most end up gaining it back. And many do feel better because toxins are removed.

A juice cleanse is also good for those who can't discontinue medication. On a water fast, the person supervising the fast will often recommend discontinuing all medication since the whole point is to cleanse the body. Remember, drugs are toxic, but some are necessary, as in the case of Type 1 diabetes. Going off medication can't always be done. In those cases, juicing is recommended, along with supervision.

What do I eat when I stop fasting?

The longer the fast, the more careful one must be when re-feeding. It's actually very simple, but it's not easy. Short fasts of a few days do not require as much forethought as fasts of one or more weeks. I never advise going back to junk food or addictions. *Ending a fast is a wonderful opportunity to start a new beginning.*

Plan ahead by researching re-feeding. Most recommend re-feeding with fruit, a little every few hours. Depending on the length of the fast, it can take a week or more. Make sure to factor in re-feeding time. For every week of fasting I add two days of re-feeding. For example, those who fast for three weeks need to incorporate an extra week for refeeding.

I know a handful of people who experienced digestive pain by jumping right back into old eating patterns or by eating too much healthy food. Most are inclined to eat too much and the wrong type of food. Don't focus on your favorite burger or pizza as the end of the fast approaches; focus on papayas, oranges, or berries for a few days. *It's often harder to control the re-entering of food than to abstain during the fast.*

Re-feeding and genuine hunger

When real hunger returns, you often don't feel sluggish, mad, or moody. The reason we often feel grumpy when a meal is missed is because we have established eating patterns. The bad "feelings" are often a sign of cleansing, and cleansing hurts. When the body is constantly fed, it has no time to detox because it's always in digestion mode. For this reason, many encourage not eating until lunchtime before breaking the nighttime fast to allow the body to detox—hence the word *break-fast*. Breaking the nighttime fast doesn't have to begin with an early meal.

When we eat and feel better, the "feeling better" occurs because the body gets a "fix," just like an addict would. The energy that was being used to detox the body is now being rerouted to digest and assimilate food. As a result, the person avoids a detox state because the process of digestion starts over again—a process we never break free from unless we fast. When we eat, and eat again, and again, we don't cleanse.

Genuine hunger is a feeling that very few actually feel in America. It says, "It's time to eat because the reserves have been depleted." It's not affected by mood swings; it is driven by biological needs. The body will tell you when it's time to eat after fasting. Most of us have never fasted long enough to feel genuine hunger return.

Who shouldn't fast?

Obviously, there are people who shouldn't fast, such as those who are emaciated or have certain illnesses or nursing or pregnant mothers. But they should be on a very clean God-given eating program while avoiding sugar-filled drinks and fast food. However, I would encourage research in this area because many illnesses are reversed during a fast.

Also, just because a person is underweight does not mean that fasting is bad for them; there are huge benefits for them too. Many studies describe how underweight people who fasted actually gained more weight after the fast because the body was cleansed and cells were rejuvenated. *Just because a person is underweight does not mean that they are healthy—their body still needs cleansing.*

Children are probably another exception to fasting. However, I knew a twelve-year-old girl who water fasted for three days and had great results. Fasting is often easier for young adults because their body is less toxic. If kids aren't hungry, don't force the issue. A lack of hunger often means they shouldn't eat right then, especially when sick. Dr. Yuri Nikolayev, mentioned earlier, was introduced to fasting as a child. When he would get sick, his mother encouraged a three-day fast.

Kids today are overfed, not underfed, and they are often under-nourished. Cavities, attention deficits, chronic sickness, anxiety, and depression are often signs of poor health in children. Add caffeinated drinks to the mix, and it becomes a recipe for failed health. *Children are rarely fed what they "need" but are often given what they "want."* Change that if you can—from school districts to church functions to your own family. Children are an incredible gift from God. Shouldn't they have health stacked in their favor?

Can I tell others that I'm fasting?

This question arises from Jesus's words in Matthew 6:18 that we should not appear to be fasting. It is a heart issue rather than an information issue. A limited amount of people, such as your spouse or friends who will encourage you, can know you're fasting, if your heart is right. After all, how did we know that people fasted in the Bible if they didn't tell anyone? Their transparency motivates us. Whereas if you're going out of your way to tell others and posting it on Facebook and Twitter, Matthew 6:18 would apply. However, God may release you after, or even during, the fast to tell others and motivate them. Pray and wait on Him for direction.

Keep in mind that most frown upon fasting largely because of wrong information. Also, people may feel "guilty" if others are fasting and they are not. Don't flaunt fasting. We need to encourage, not discourage, people, and read Isaiah 58 often.

I usually try to avoid the subject around others unless I'm leading the church on a corporate fast. When someone says, "You look skinny. Are you sick? Why are you starving yourself?" We can respond, "I'm not starving myself; I'm feeding my spirit, recapturing my health, and feeling good in the process." It is sometimes those who stop by McDonald's and Starbucks who feel the need to lecture others about fasting. *The question shouldn't be "Why are you fasting?" but rather "Why aren't you fasting?"*

When should I fast?

Opinions are mixed, but my personal belief is:

- *When the Lord leads you to fast.* When this occurs, the conviction is that it's time to starve the flesh and seek God.

- *When you're feeling spiritually drained.* When Jesus said, "When you pray and give," He also said, "When you fast" (Matt. 6). When something is expected by the Lord, it's wise to do it often.

- *Before taking on a huge task or when making an important decision.* Moses received the Ten Commandments. King Jehoshaphat experienced victory. Elijah was restored. Ezra received direction and protection. Esther was saved, along with her people. Nehemiah was strengthened. Jesus was empowered. And on and on it goes. The history of God moving when men and women fast is seen all throughout Scripture.

- *When feeling sick, tired, or sluggish or if you need to lose weight.* I get cold very easily when fasting and my strength comes and goes. One must plan accordingly and take a few days off to rest. Weekends work well.

- *Once a week.* Since we often don't "feel" like fasting, we can't always wait for a feeling—be preventive instead of reactive. After we consume our last evening meal, the body begins to digest and assimilate. Don't eat right before bed, if possible, and don't be in a hurry to eat in the morning. Give the digestive tract a break as often as possible.

History shows that light eaters who are not overweight live the longest and have the most productive lives. *Fasting is a lifestyle, not a fad.*

How you fast is just as important as when you fast

Isaiah 58:3 says, "'Why have we fasted,' they say, 'and You have not seen? Why have we afflicted our souls, and You take no notice?'" In short, because their fast lacked obedience, it was fruitless. If you're holding on to sin, remaining bitter and arrogant, taking advantage of people, or gossiping, backbiting, and hurting others, fasting may do little for you. For the believer, sin must be covered with repentance to release the full potential of fasting. Spiritually speaking, you can't fast from food and still feed sin. Turn off negative media and other distractions. The key to fasting is humility—the releasing of appetite must correspond with the releasing of sin. In Isaiah 58:9 we read these encouraging words: "Then you shall call, and the Lord will answer." Although God still hears our prayers even when we don't fast (we launched a church and began a ministry without fasting), fasting draws us closer to God and makes us more sensitive to His will.

Do we really believe that we are walking in the fullness of our God-given potential? Fasting expands that horizon. The door of possibilities enlarges, and the power of the Spirit is magnified. *Jesus "returned in the power of the Spirit" after fasting, and so can you.*

PART THREE
Feasting—What to Eat and Why

The Problem Hasn't Changed

We are at the crossroads: Opioid and alcohol abuse are leaving a path of destruction in their wake; obesity is escalating, plaguing the young as well as the old, reaching epidemic levels in children; diabetes is affecting millions; and cancer and heart disease are the number one killers in America. Are there answers? Yes—if we look to God's Word.

Although I believed that I was healthy and fit, by the time I reached my 22nd birthday, my 6'2" frame had skyrocketed to over 270 pounds. I was diagnosed with borderline hypoglycemia. My blood pressure and cholesterol levels were high, and my health was rapidly deteriorating. I was told that I might need to take medication for the rest of my life. I was shocked! **I knew that if I didn't change my lifestyle, my lifestyle would change me!**

In the late '90s, long before I became a pastor, I was a corporate executive for 24 Hour Fitness. I managed fitness centers while assisting and interviewing thousands of weight-loss clients. As a result, I identified a consistent pattern that surfaced time and time again. In 2001, I wrote a book about these patterns entitled *What Works When "Diets" Don't.* Rodney Corn, then Director of Education, Research, and Development for the National Academy of Sports Medicine, was gracious enough to endorse it: "Shane Idleman has captured the true essence of weight-loss! His concise application for getting to the root of weight problems sheds a much-needed new light on taking control over both the physical and spiritual aspects of weight-loss."

Although the root problem hasn't changed, much has changed in our understanding of nutrition in the last few decades. If I could rewrite that book, I would make a few corrections. For one, I wouldn't focus as much on counting calories. Although it's important for people to be aware of calorie-dense foods, it can become burdensome. Second, I didn't include fasting, but I should have. Third, I wouldn't promote as much carbohydrate intake as I did then. As our society becomes increasingly more sedentary, we need to be strategic.

Herein lies the main problem we face today: *There isn't a consensus on what exactly we should be eating to maintain health.* Some experts promote only plant-based diets, while others say that clean meat and raw dairy must be staples. Many authorities encourage high fruit consumption, whereas others embrace high fat diets. Proponents of five meals a day stand in stark contrast to athletes who claim to eat just twice a day. One fasting expert only eats fruit and claims he has not been sick in over 25 years. On the other hand, many well-known nutritionists are adamant about ketogenic diets that are often high in animal protein and fat, yet there are vegetarian versions as well. Who is right?

Confusion leads to discouragement, which leads to failure, but are there answers? Does the Bible have anything to say about a healthy diet? I think it does, but I'm not prescribing a diet; I'm prescribing a lifestyle. We must look at food as stewardship, not being mastered by what we consume (1 Cor. 10:23). Hopefully, the following pages will point you in the right direction.

Does God Care about What We Eat?

Food should primarily be about fuel and stewardship, followed by enjoyment. In America, it's all about enjoyment. I don't agree with those who say, "God doesn't care about what we eat." How can He not care about one of the major contributors to disease nor be concerned about addictive and destructive ingredients? **How can He not care about something that greatly affects our children as well as our performance, health, and vitality?** Often, that statement about God not caring is just an excuse to indulge, or a lack of wisdom. God wants us to take care of His gift; it matters. Let's briefly look at His design.

A calorie is a unit of energy derived from food. The energy comes from three main sources: *carbohydrates* (a quick source of energy), *fats* (an essential nutrient for life-sustaining functions as well as an energy source), and *proteins* (essential for building and repairing tissue, it can also be used as an energy source if other means are not available). All three are important for good health.

Carbohydrates are currently at the forefront of most diet discussions. They consist of foods that originate from the ground and foods developed by man. Many people choose the wrong type of carbohydrates, those developed by man: sweets, processed foods, soft drinks, pastries, white flour products, and so on. Unbelievably, some of the chemicals used in these processed foods are banned in Europe.

Poor food choices are one reason why we see so many cavities in the young as well as the old. It's not just the harmful ingredients that cause damage, it's the lack of vitamins, minerals, and nutrients that teeth need. I've seen cavities heal when a proper diet is introduced and harmful foods removed.

Our bodies are designed to consume healthy, God-given carbohydrates such as colorful fruits and vegetables along with beans and yams. Years ago, when I worked in construction, I could eat more carbohydrates than I do now. We must be strategic based on our lifestyle; some carbohydrates are important for living a healthy life.

After carbohydrates are consumed, they are broken down into glucose. One of *three* processes occur: 1) The glucose will serve an immediate need such as exercise or activity or assist in recovery; 2) if there is no immediate need, glucose is stored in the muscle and the liver for future use; or 3) if the liver and muscles are full, the glucose will be converted into fat and stored for future use.

The storage capacity in the liver is rather small; it supplies energy to the brain and the central nervous system, whereas the storage capacity in the muscle is larger. More muscle means more storage capacity. Here is the main problem: *Weight gain and health problems occur when too many calories, especially the wrong ones, are consumed and not used.*

Special note: When I use the word *refined*, it means that nutrients are removed and chemicals are added, especially in the case of oils. Refined vegetable oils are often sold in bulk and end up in many prepackaged food items—even healthy ones. Once heated to high temperatures, they are then processed with petroleum solvents and heated again to remove waxy build up. More chemicals are then added to remove the smell. Long term, they can wreak havoc on our body and fuel both disease and inflammation. Many attribute heart disease to refined vegetable oils for this very reason. **Whether it's sugar, refined oils, or processed food, junk is the main problem.**

(As a side note: If decision makers who oversee food corporations, even "healthy" ones, read this, would you please consider using healthy ingredients, even if it affects profit?)

I'm a proponent of eating the actual food versus using the oil. When possible, I use olives instead of olive oil, avocados instead of avocado oil, and almonds instead of almond oil. Choose sources such as avocados and nuts in salad or flax seeds in steel-cut organic oatmeal. *Not only is the breakdown of the food slower (e.g., low glycemic), the uptake of nutrients and fiber is substantially higher when eating the whole food.*

Oils to avoid

Current research supports avoiding foods, even healthy ones, that contain palm, sunflower, canola, corn, soybean, peanut, safflower, or cottonseed oil as well as foods containing partially hydrogenated and hydrogenated oils. This can be challenging. It's hard to even locate healthy peanut butter without refined oils.[19]

---

[19] EatThis.com compares different peanut butter brands and recommends the healthiest at http://www.eatthis.com/peanut-butter-ranked.

Sadly, most of the organic products on the market today contain refined oils. I switched from organic to homemade hummus for this very reason. When possible, use oils in their natural state, such as coconut oil or olive oil. Grapeseed oil is somewhat controversial; many believe the high omega-6 qualities can create inflammation if not balanced with omega-3. If you go this route, use it in moderation and buy organic and unrefined.

Keep in mind that terms such as *organic, natural, GMO free, vegan, no trans-fats*, and others are often used for marketing purposes. For example, many popular brands of chips are switching ingredients around so they can place the word *organic* on their packaging, but the product is far from healthy. There are exceptions, but generally, not all products labeled *natural* or *organic* are healthy. As Food and Water Watch notes:

> Right now the most meaningful label on your food, in terms of upholding specific government requirements, is the U.S. Department of Agriculture (USDA) organic seal. For a product to be certified organic, it's required to meet specific standards:
> Organic crops cannot be grown with synthetic fertilizers, synthetic pesticides or sewage sludge.
> Organic crops cannot be genetically engineered or irradiated.
> Animals must eat only organically grown feed ... and can't be treated with synthetic hormones or antibiotics.
> Animals must have access to the outdoors. ...
> Animals cannot be cloned.[20]

Many people are not concerned about food additives or ingredients because they believe the FDA offers protection. That's simply not the case. **The FDA is no longer an organization focused on prevention but on reaction.** In other words, the food products in our nation are too numerous for the FDA to regulate; therefore, most of the supervision is left to the companies that are producing the products. As a result, the FDA must react to health concerns, not prevent them. You be the judge! Rather

---

[20] "Understanding Food Labels," Food & Water Watch, https://www.foodand waterwatch.org/about/live-healthy/consumer-labels. This article will help you understand food labels and what certain terms, such as *certified organic*, mean.

than a neutral agency testing without bias, production companies have profit at stake.

Back to carbohydrates. When consumed in moderation and in the right forms such as beans, carbohydrates have many benefits. Dr. Joel Fuhrman adds, "Bean intake recurs in scientific studies as an important factor promoting long life. The conclusions of an important longitudinal study show that a higher legume intake is the most protective dietary predictor of survival among the elderly, regardless of their ethnicity."[21]

Consuming too many carbohydrates, especially the wrong kinds, causes weight gain and has a negative effect on health, largely because they lack nutrients. Yet a person would have a difficult time eating too many green vegetables, one of the most nutrient-dense foods on the planet.

The goal is to consume nutrient-dense food such as fruits and vegetables at every meal. Ironically, those with the highest amounts of nutrients, like broccoli, are often the lowest in calories. When you consume nutrient-dense food, cravings for sweets will decrease.

On average, individuals in our culture consume a great deal of calories from refined sugar. Whether the source is a candy bar, a protein bar, or a vegan cookie, it's still sugar. These large doses are frequently responsible for failing health and obesity. Fruit, when eaten in moderation, is a much better choice. This is another reason why fasting is so important; it rebalances, restores, and renews the body.

Dr. Rex Russell offers three principles when considering sugar: 1) Eat sugar in the items God created for food such as fruit and honey; 2) eat the items before they are altered and changed into toxic products such as donuts or candy bars; and 3) if you are becoming addicted, cut back substantially.[22] Manuka honey is a great choice; it's an antioxidant

---

[21] Dr. Fuhrman has numerous videos and articles online. This is one regarding the benefits of beans: https://elegantbeans.com/joel-fuhrman-beans-lead-to-longer-life.

[22] Rex Russell, *What the Bible Says about Healthy Living* (Grand Rapids: Revell, 1996), 160.

powerhouse. I add a teaspoon to protein shakes when needed. Manuka honey is said to be one of the most beneficial forms of honey in the world.

One soft drink can contain up to 40 grams of refined sugar and 150 calories. *Theoretically, you could lose one pound a week by doing nothing more than deleting three-fourths of the refined, unhealthy sugar from your diet.* There are also studies concluding that even moderate sugar intake hinders the immune system from fighting illness, including heart disease.

Can we blame all carbohydrates for our nation's weight problem? Many do. As a result, low-carbohydrate diets have become popular. Most of these diets exclude whole grains and fruit and only allow vegetables, meat, and dairy. But many still agree that overall calorie consumption determines weight gain. Try not eating for a week and see what happens. However, I agree that carbohydrates such as white bread, rice, pastries, candy, soft drinks, and processed food should be minimized, if not eliminated. Health should always be the central factor when choosing a food or health program. **Without health, especially spiritual health, a trim body has little significance!**

When carbohydrates are consumed, insulin is released in the blood to transport the energy into the cells. Insulin is a hormone that forces cells to absorb glucose for energy. Though necessary, the more insulin we have, the harder it is to lose weight and maintain health. If the body doesn't use the glucose that's being transported, it is stored as excessive energy (fat). When overburdened by too much sugar or carbohydrates, the cells become resistant to insulin. As a result, glucose collects in the blood, and an array of health issues can result.

I recently heard that a large milkshake featured at a popular drive-through establishment contains an incredible 93 grams of sugar—approximately 23 teaspoons of sugar. And we wonder why poor health is robbing us of life. Additionally, for cells to uptake sufficient amounts of vitamin C, large amounts of sugar cannot be present since sugar competes with vitamin C to enter the cell. **Now you see why so many people are deficient in key vitamins and minerals—they are addicted to the bad things and avoid the good things.**

More on fat

There are close to 55 grams of fat in a double-bacon cheeseburger, compared to 10 in a lean meat patty. To burn the 1,100 calories in the burger, it would take a 2½ hour bike ride—and the burger is probably loaded with harmful ingredients.

Fat is stored for energy, helps the body absorb necessary fat-soluble vitamins, and protects organs. It also affects brain development and helps with inflammation. Processed fat, such as hydrogenated and partially hydrogenated oils, are hard on the system, as are most vegetable oils in chips, cookies, and pastries. It makes me wonder: Do we really have a cholesterol problem that stems from healthy animal products or a refined oil, sugar, and carbohydrate problem? Could it be that junk food is what causes severe inflammation in the arteries?

Nicole Eckert drove this point home in an article entitled "Heart Surgeon Speaks Out About the True Cause of Heart Disease." She writes:

> Take a moment and picture a fresh pad of steel wool. Now visualize yourself slowly rubbing this abrasive sponge over your soft skin until it becomes tender, red and nearly bleeding.
> If you could tolerate this form of pain and repeated the action, the area would swell, bleed and become infected after the repeated harm.
> This uncomfortable visualization is a good way to conceptualize the inflammatory process that could be taking place inside your body right now.[23]

When inflammation occurs, cholesterol via low-density lipoproteins (LDL) come to the rescue but are then blamed for the heart disease. I heard Dr. Axe make similar comparisons. **God didn't create "bad" cholesterol; man created "bad" food.** Additionally, eating cholesterol does not necessarily raise blood cholesterol. As *Harvard Health Publishing* notes, "If you eat only 200 to 300 milligrams (mg) of cholesterol a day (one egg yolk

---

[23] Nicole Eckert, Healthy Holistic Living, http://www.healthy-holistic-living.com/heart-surgeon-speaks-true-cause-heart-disease.html. Read the article to learn about how inflammation affects the body and what steps can be taken.

has about 200 mg), your liver will produce an additional 800 milligrams per day from raw materials such as fat, sugars, and proteins."[24]

Our motto 20 years ago was "Eat less—move more." Now it's "Eat right—move a lot more." Movement, like fasting, is natural medicine. There is truth in the statement "If you don't use it, you lose it." Muscle deteriorates, cells are damaged, and joints become crystallized when not used or fed the right diet.

As you can see, we have a storage problem, a moving problem, and a problem making wise choices. If a person is 20 pounds overweight, technically they have close to 70,000 calories in storage to burn. This person could fast for over three weeks on water alone, but instead, most people consume too much and burden the body on a regular basis.

What Does the Bible Say about Food?

There are many views regarding what diet is ideal. Vegans, vegetarians, proponents of plant-based diets, and meat promoters all argue that their diet is best. Throw the raw diet crowd into the mix, and the confusion only increases. Many of these diets overlap but with some stark differences. For example, hard-core raw advocates don't cook any food. They consume it straight from the tree, vine, or ground. Plant-based diets promote raw, but they are often flexible and have a much broader range of choices.

I don't claim to have all the answers. Even experts in the field of nutrition are divided, but again, we can glean a great deal from the biblical account. **Most diets are written from an evolutionary perspective, so it's important that we get our facts straight.** So let's begin where God begins.

In the beginning of creation, God said:

> "Behold, I have given you every plant yielding seed that is on the surface of all the earth, and every tree which has fruit yielding seed; it shall be food for you; and to every beast of the earth and

---

[24] "How it's Made: Cholesterol production in your body," *Harvard Health Publishing*, Harvard Medical School, https://www.health.harvard.edu/heart-health/how-its-made-cholesterol-production-in-your-body.

to every bird of the sky and to every thing that moves on the earth which has life, I have given every green plant for food"; and it was so. (Gen. 1:29–30 NASB)

We were designed to eat living, plant-based food. The life of the plant via vitamins, minerals, and enzymes is to be deposited into the body—to restore, renew, and replenish. We read that, after the flood, everything that lives and moves was to be food for us except the blood that is in the animal (Gen. 9:3). The blood of an animal contains toxins. Many diseases travel in the blood. God also identified clean and unclean animals. Un-clean animals, such as pork, are still not considered healthy since viruses, bacteria, and parasites are easily transferred from the pig to us.

Was man not to consume meat until after the flood, approximately 1,600 years after the fall? If so, why? Did early man eat only plants for over 16 centuries before God allowed meat?[25] How did a plant-based diet provide vitamin B12, calcium, iron, and zinc when they are difficult to obtain in a plant-based diet? Is it permissible to eat meat and dairy but not ideal? Should it be consumed sparingly? Does it balance nature (i.e., kill and eat)?

Biblically speaking, you can find support for a few different views, but we are encouraged to let our moderation be known to all men. Moderation means drinking or eating something *occasionally*. Unfortunately, moderation is often abused, and very unhealthy patterns develop. Paul said all things may be allowed, but all things are not beneficial (1 Cor. 10:23). In most areas where people live the longest, their diets are primarily plant-based.

I believe that the pre-flood atmosphere of the earth was much different than our living conditions today. Man lived in a healthier environment that may have provided more oxygen and greater protection against the harmful rays of the sun, and plants and fruit-bearing trees grew in abundance. After the flood, however, fruits and vegetables became scarce (see Gen. 8:22: seedtime and harvest). I believe that God allowed meat consumption because of this scarcity. Healthy meat and dairy can be

---

[25] Answers in Genesis provides a well-documented chart entitled "Timeline for the Flood" at https://answersingenesis.org/bible-timeline/timeline-for-the-flood.

enjoyed from time to time for those who want to go this route, but it shouldn't be consumed in abundance. *Personally, I'd rather err on the side of eating what we ate before the fall as my primary source of nutrition.* But again, this is my opinion.

A few Scriptures to consider:

- In Ezekiel 4:9, we read that Ezekiel was to take "wheat, barley, beans, lentils, millet, and spelt . . . and make bread." This was his diet for over a year. Was it for convenience sake or health sake? We can only speculate, but this plant combination had/has many health benefits.

- In Daniel 1, Daniel ate vegetables and water for 10 days and looked better than those who ate meat and delicacies. Plant food brings life (Rev. 22:2). It should be our primary focus at every meal.

- In Daniel 10, it appears that he did this again for 21 days. The spiritual outcome was incredible. I find it interesting that God blesses fasts where only vegetables are consumed.

- Meat aligns more with our animalistic nature; cravings for meat have been the downfall of many (see Num. 11). People were often rebuked because of gluttony over meat.

- When God fed the children of Israel in the wilderness, He provided "bread from heaven" known as manna (Ex. 16:4; John 6:31). The people made it into cakes or boiled it. It had the appearance of bdellium (from trees). The Bible states the manna tasted like wafers made with honey. The perfect food that God chose appears to be plant-based, not meat-based. This is rather compelling for me. Then God brought in millions of quail because the people "lusted for meat."

- But in Acts 10, we find that Peter had a vision in which God instructed him to kill and eat meat.

- In Romans 14:1–2, the apostle Paul talks about not judging a person who eats meat. Granted, this could be referring to the unclean nature of certain foods and whether those foods were offered to idols rather than being a proof text for meat-based diets.

- In 1 Timothy 4:3–4, Paul said that in the last days deceiving spirits will command people to abstain from certain foods—foods which God created to be received with thanksgiving. This verse is one reason why I don't prohibit any food that God created for food, including healthy meat and dairy.

Be careful when making absolute and dogmatic statements about diet. However, we can be assured that *healthy* is the way to go. Living food places vitamins, minerals, and powerful phytochemicals directly into the body. *Man-made food is dead; it doesn't give—it takes.*

My Thoughts on the Disease Epidemic

After pouring over many articles, documentaries, and health plans, I narrowed down what may be fueling our disease epidemic. Clearly, something happened to our DNA as the result of the fall—whether it's cells only being able to duplicate a certain amount of times, or sin allowing the mutation of DNA sequencing, something catastrophic happened. The question is: Do we fuel disease and strengthen its grip by making poor choices, or do we fight it by making wise choices? Granted, we live in a fallen world that often results in illness and disease. We can't always prevent that.

Let's look at what a day for a typical Christian might look like:

The day may begin with unhealthy cereal and milk, along with sugar water—that is, pasteurized orange juice. Or we may grab a large cup of coffee as we frantically run out the door. Sadly, there is little time for God.

We fail to get adequate sleep as well as adequate amounts of water. Contrary to popular thought, the body cannot acquire restful sleep after consuming caffeine. The only reason a person can fall asleep after consuming it is because of sheer exhaustion. With caffeine in the system, deep sleep vital to health and recovery remains elusive; therefore, we wake up exhausted instead of refreshed.

Lunch may consist of fast food or a "healthy" turkey sandwich containing sodium nitrates in the meat, processed bread, and nutrient-deficient cheese. We may also purchase a bag of so-called healthy chips and a drink loaded with sugar.

We come home exhausted and quickly prepare a large piece of meat with heaps of pasta and a few pieces of limp broccoli for dinner. We spend the next few hours watching mindless entertainment while eating sugary sweets.

It's a never-ending cycle of fatigue and stress that manifests itself in physical and mental illness, weight gain, and overall poor health. Think of what we are doing to our children by laying this unhealthy foundation early in their lives. It's time to break this cycle!

Disease often prevails when the bad guys are fed and the good guys are starved. Oxidative stress is the battle in our body between free radicals (terrorists) and the antioxidants (good guys). The constant bombardment wears the body down, hence the words "oxidative stress." Antioxidants found in living food are like the Army, Navy, Air Force, and Marines. Antioxidants disarm the free-radical terrorists by donating electrons to them. They become stable rather than radical.

A Quick Recap

Here are five ways we can fuel disease based on what we have covered so far:

1. Unhealthy meat is a toxic choice if we factor in growth hormones, antibiotics, drug residue, pathogens, worms, biotoxins, and carcinogens from packaging as well as cooking. And most dairy products have been tainted and altered. If poor choices are made in this area, more terrorists are deployed into the body. **I'm not against healthy meat and dairy in moderation; I'm against toxic meat and dairy in abundance.** In countries like Austria and France and in areas near the Mediterranean, heart disease is much lower than in America, even though they eat more fat. We must look at all factors that cause inflammation and disease. Most antioxidants found in meat and dairy come from the nutrient-rich plants that the animals eat. If animals are fed genetically modified feed with zero life-giving benefits and injected with hormones and antibiotics, these factors will lower their antioxidant output.

2. If high levels of sugar, such as high fructose corn syrup, dextrose, maltose, rice syrup, sucrose, and dozens more, are added to the terrorism team, the strength of the enemy grows. Increased levels of

sugar intake, along with a substantial rise in meat or dairy consumption, could be one possible link to cancer—the one-two punch. Dr. Joel Fuhrman has noted this as well.[26] High sugar intake releases insulin into the bloodstream, and high levels of animal protein consumption can raise *insulin-like growth factor 1* (IGF-1). IGF-1 is a hormone that is similar to insulin. It joins with *growth hormone* to reproduce and regenerate cells. *This is great news if the cells are healthy but bad news if they are cancerous.* **In short, excess sugar sparks the flame of disease, and the abundant IGF-1 throws gas on the fire.** (Also avoid fake sweeteners such as aspartame, which is also known as AminoSweet, Nutrasweet, and Equal, at all costs. They are chemicals, not natural sweeteners.)

3. If we add refined vegetable oils to the terrorism team, arteries and healthy cells become damaged due to inflammation.

4. Add the failure to fast to the equation and the enemy gains additional ground. Fasting invites *SEAL Team Six* to the battle. Among other things, fasting starves the fuel source of free radicals because most toxins are released during the digestion of food. Imagine what a bowl of junk cereal releases into your body compared to nothing being released when fasting. **I believe that fasting slows aging for this very reason: It minimizes toxins while allowing the body to cleanse and rebuild.** Granted, fasting will cause the body to release stored toxins as part of the cleansing process, but the body is prepared for this.

5. Throw inactivity into the battle, and the terrorists gain even more strength. Our bodies were not designed to sit for long periods of time. In 2006, Harvard Medical School made the following statement: "Exercise helps prevent atherosclerosis. It keeps arteries healthy by lowering LDL ("bad") cholesterol and boosting HDL ("good") cholesterol. And it also helps by improving other atherosclerotic risk factors such as high blood pressure, diabetes, obesity, stress, and

---

[26] Dr. Joel Fuhrman comes to this same conclusion regarding meat and sugar. He breaks it down in this YouTube video I highly recommend watching: "The End of Dieting, How to Prevent Disease by Joel Fuhrman MD."

various other factors that promote blood clots."[27] Inactivity often leads to weight gain and sluggish blood flow. **Remember that every pound of fat requires a few extra miles of blood vessels.** That means more work for the body, especially the heart. Lose the excess and bring in more reinforcements.

Time does not allow me to write about additional factors such as stress, a lack of deep sleep, and living in a toxic world. Research the effects of stress on the body as well as how sleep affects health. If we combine all these factors, it's easy to see why disease has reached epidemic levels. Work on these areas, and you can change the course of the battle in your favor.

More on Meat, Dairy, Moderation, and Finances

Just as we are permitted to consume meat and dairy, we are also permitted to drink alcohol—but we all know about the devastating consequences of overconsumption. **Does the same principle of moderation apply to meat and dairy?** Granted, meat and dairy advocates such as Weston A. Price have impressive data showing how people have thrived on healthy meat and raw dairy. There are healthy tribes of people eating plant-based food and other villages, such as in the Himalayas, who eat raw dairy and unprocessed meat; both groups are healthy. The key is that the food is not toxic or sugar-ladened. Ironically, as I was writing this section, WebMD released this news: "Researchers found that just a 10% increase in ultra-processed foods led to a 12% higher risk of cancer."[28] **We reap what we sow. What are we sowing?**

---

[27] "Exercise and your arteries" Harvard Health Publishing, Harvard Medical School, https://www.health.harvard.edu/newsletter_article/Exercise_and_your_art eries.

[28] "Highly Processed Foods Tied to Higher Cancer Risk," WebMD, https://www.webmd.com/cancer/news/20180214/highly-processed-foods-tied-to- higher-cancer-risk. Ultra-processed food intake was measured against breast, prostate, and colorectal cancer. Read more at "Ultra-processed foods linked to increased cancer risk" on CNN.com.

If you choose the route of dairy in moderation, there is compelling research supporting raw cow and goat milk. Many argue that pasteurization kills just about everything good. In August 2016, Vicki Batts wrote an impressive article for raw dairy advocates. Here is an excerpt:

> The *Journal of Allergy and Clinical Immunology* has shown that consuming raw milk will not, in fact, be a death sentence. Researchers, doctors and other medical professionals from across Europe joined forces to investigate the effects of consuming raw milk, and revealed that raw milk isn't just non-toxic, but also yields some impressive health benefits! ... Essentially, raw milk helps to decrease inflammation, while processed milk creates *more* inflammation.[29]

Many say that raw milk and honey are complete foods. It's interesting that God told His people that He would give them a land "flowing with milk and honey" (Ex. 33:3).

A quick note about raw dairy

As with vaccines, research both sides, and come to your own conclusion. Some say that the pasteurization process is designed to protect people from certain diseases and that it does not significantly reduce the nutritional content, but others disagree. When certain foods are heated, they do lose nutritional benefits, but just how much is the question. I've seen a stark contrast in the magnified images of raw milk compared to pasteurized milk. The nutrients in the pasteurized milk appeared damaged, if not dead. For your convenience two opposing views are footnoted.[30] **I find it ironic that many who are against raw dairy have no problem consuming raw sushi.**

---

[29] "The evidence is in: Raw milk actually boosts immunity, prevents infections," NewsTarget, http://www.newstarget.com/2016-08-15-the-evidence-is-in-raw-milk -actually-boosts-immunity-prevents-infections.html (emphasis in original).

[30] Dr. Robert Irons earned his PhD in Nutritional Immunology from the University of Missouri-Columbia. His article can be found in the article "Pasteurization Does Harm Real Milk" on RealMilk.com. Livestrong.com published their view with the article "Does Pasteurization Kill Nutrients?"

Common Objections

Some may argue, "This is too hard; it really limits my diet." You are correct. Nothing worth having comes easily, including good health. But is it really that hard when compared to those who lived hundreds or thousands of years ago who had to hunt and gather their food and put everything together? In the past, one meal could take hours to prepare. We should be thankful; we have it easy compared to past generations.

"It's too expensive," complains another. True, it is expensive, but so is cancer, open heart surgery, and chronic illness. Can we really put a price tag on good health? I mentioned stewardship at the beginning for this reason—it must come before enjoyment. I recently compared organic produce with other brands. Organic carrots were $1.99 for a two-pound bag versus $1.49 for non-organic. Organic apples were $1 more per pound than non-organic. The difference wasn't significant since excluding meat and junk food that day saved me $30. Granted, organic produce is not bulletproof, but it is a better choice when possible.

Parents, we should fight for the health of our children, not contribute to their poor health. We are setting them up for failure be-fore they even begin. It's hard, but it can be done. When the pantry and the refrigerator contain only good food, guess what the kids will eat? A "treat" now and then should not be a "staple" in our homes. Yes, they will complain, but eventually, they'll ask for carrots and apples. Nursing moms, your diet will greatly affect the quality of life-giving milk. Choose wisely.

Again, I'm not talking about perfection but direction. I don't know anyone who eats perfectly, and our family is no exception; it's a daily struggle. As one example, we hosted a homeless outreach at our church in the winter, and our staff ate dinner with them. I ate pizza one evening and fried chicken the next. Granted, our homeless and low-income brothers and sisters need healthy food just as much as us. Looking back, I should have promoted healthy food the week we fed them.

When it comes to finances, it's all about priorities. Ending a coffee habit saved one man $200 a month. Another saved $400 when he stopped smoking and eating fast food for lunch. I knew one family who spent over $800 a month eating out. Granted, some families are truly constrained. Do the best with what you have, and God will honor that, but choose the right foods when possible. Avoid the junk food in the checkout line and down the middle aisles of most grocery stores. In general, vegetables are cheaper than meat. **Cheap food is often not good food.**

Again, in answering the questions presented in the subtitle, *What Works, What Doesn't, and Why*, it's very simple. What works? God's design and biblical principles work. What doesn't work? Neither fitness obsession nor indifference toward physical health work—both are harmful. Why do God's principles succeed? They are guardrails through the canyons of life. They don't prevent us from experiencing pleasure; they protect us from falling.

To Whom Are You Listening?

As we learned, the perversion and altering of food is what causes damage; it takes the life, nutrition, and health out of the food. Sadly, most are still listening to the world's influence about what to eat. We are bombarded by commercials and surrounded by fast food establishments. The influence is also affecting the church. We serve donuts instead of fruit. We promote chili cook-offs but not events to work it off. Hundreds show up for potlucks, but very few for prayer and fasting services. *Why do we pray for wisdom in other areas but not in the area of health and nutrition?* Where are you getting your information from? Whom are you trusting? Take time today and read Psalm 1.

Do we have a gluten, allergy, or carbohydrate problem, or do we have a pesticide, poison, and chemical problem? The common denominator in the different programs such as *Forks Over Knives*, *Paleo*, and *The Ketogenic Diet* is often the promotion of a healthy lifestyle and diet. Most of them eliminate junk food that is man-made and man-manipulated.

In *Forks Over Knives*, I'd be curious to know if they also tested meat that was pure, unaltered, and organic, or did the meat contain antibiotics, hormones, and chemicals? Did their conclusions factor in those who eat healthy meat and dairy in moderation or in abundance?

Regarding dairy, could it have also been the aflatoxin in the study on rats that caused cancer and not just the casein protein in the milk? What about the sugar and the IGF-1 connection mentioned earlier? Was the casein pure and clean, or was it taken from a toxic source? Were the cows that produced the casein fed grain that was loaded with pesticides and toxic chemicals? I don't necessarily disagree with the findings, but I do have many questions.

I was surprised that this documentary didn't encourage produce that was organic and free of chemicals, as if animal fat is bad but harmful chemicals are neutral. Dr. Caldwell Esselstyn was gracious enough to talk to me in March 2018 about this. He explained that chemicals were not the focus of the study.

Who is right and who is wrong? **The meat and dairy industry has lobbyists, documentaries have agendas, and publishers sell for profit.** We must educate ourselves and look to God's Word for answers rather than to diets with evolutionary spins or agendas. I decided to find out what I could by comparing my blood results in a before-and-after panel. The results are included in Part 5 of this book.

Most diets do not take God's design into consideration. Granted, we are what we eat. If we eat meat, we must choose wisely and consume it in moderation. If we eat vegetables and fruit sprayed with toxic chemicals, they will enter our body. If we eat too much sugar, we will pay the price as well.

Take time this week and research the effects of sugar on the body—you will be amazed at the damage it causes. At last count, there were 56 different names for sugar. In the year 1800, it was estimated that the average person consumed 5 to 6 teaspoons a day. This number is what I aim for each day—not each meal. I typically will have a large vegan cookie and a small piece of healthy chocolate sweetened with coconut sugar. (For reference, a large donut contains 6 teaspoons, or 24 grams.) In 1900, the average person consumed around 27 teaspoons. By 2009, 50 percent of Americans consumed approximately 56 teaspoons a day! And we wonder why there is a health crisis. *On average, we went from 1 large donut a day to 10.* If we add alcohol, medications, caffeine, and nicotine into the equation, our body becomes a ticking time bomb.

Disease is on the rise because we are deficient in the things that actually fight it, and we lack vital information about maintaining good health. I have great respect for physicians—we need them—but they are often taught how to respond with medication rather than nutrition, to treat the symptom rather than the cause. For example, the current protocol is to take statin drugs for cholesterol and blood pressure problems. But healthy levels can be achieved with proper exercise, weight loss, and good nutrition without the side effects of statins.[31] As another example, doctors often say, "Take this for your anxiety," but why not look at key lifestyle factors instead? Or, "Take this drug for Type 2 diabetes," but why not reverse the disease through proper nutrition and weight loss.

As stated before, when men age they often hear, "Take this steroid to increase testosterone." Hormone therapy may be needed now and then, but why not first offer men healthy alternatives that boost testosterone naturally? There are side effects to taking hormones such as increased anger, blood clots, heart attack, stroke, breast and prostate enlargement, and infertility, and the list continues. **We can't place all the blame on physicians; they are trained to treat, not cure and prevent. The bulk of responsibility falls on our shoulders.**

---

[31] This article, "Heart Surgeon Speaks Out About the True Cause of Heart Disease," was mentioned in Part 3. Nicole Eckert, Healthy Holistic Living, http://www.healthy-holistic-living.com/heart-surgeon-speaks-true-cause-heart-disease.html. See also "New Cholesterol Guidelines May Put 13 Million More on Statin Drugs" at Mercola.com.

PART FOUR
My Fasting Experience

22 Days of Mountains and Valleys

My hope is that my experience can motivate readers to personalize their own fast. Interwoven throughout this section is additional information about fasting and how it affects the body. Although I don't believe we should concentrate on weight, I did include my weight to show another effect of fasting.

Keep in mind that my experience may differ from yours. Fasting is a discipline that takes time to develop. Focus on intimacy with God, not on weight loss, rules, or competitions. Recall my earlier analogy: Imagine heading to lunch in a crowded mall. Just before leaving, you notice that your three-year-old has disappeared—panic sets in! You will find your child at any cost. Are you going to eat first? Of course not. The passion to find your child is far greater than the desire to eat. That's exactly what fasting is. **The desire to seek God is greater than the desire to eat.**

There were hiccups and a few setbacks during my 22-day experience, but it led to an incredible victory. The church benefited as did my family and my marriage. My spiritual and physical health was transformed, but the lows definitely matched the highs. The journaling that follows might appear meticulous, but I want to better assist the reader.

Week One

My starting weight was near 204 lbs. During this week, I began with a very clean, low-calorie diet for three days, followed by water fasting for four days. At this point, I still hung on to my morning coffee habit because I was tired and sluggish—I hoped that God would bless my fast even though I wasn't willing to give up my favorite addiction. Central nervous stimulants like coffee produce in me, and in most people, everything but the fruit of the Spirit—anger replaces love, moodiness replaces joy, and irritability replaces patience. We should also use fasting as an opportunity to fast from addictions, but we should prepare for withdrawals. For this reason, I recommend a good detox diet prior to fasting.

Try to get adequate sunlight to increase vitamin D as well as fresh air and open ventilation whenever possible. Also, be sensitive to what hair products, deodorant, and lotion you put on your skin. Your skin will absorb chemicals. During a fast, body odor and a foul taste in your mouth are signs that the body is cleansing.

I didn't see many improvements the first week because I stayed on light food for the first few days, but my voice became hoarse and sores formed in my mouth. I simply viewed this as detox. On day six, I found myself worshiping God more; fasting and prayer set the tone.

Week Two

Going into week two, my weight was 198 lbs. An increasingly painful toothache caused me to resume eating for a few days. I ate a few light meals each day from plant-based food. My right knee and other joints started to feel better, but a deep pain came first. *Before the body heals, it often hurts.* That's why riding out a fast can be beneficial.

Many are surprised that they are not on a constant spiritual high while fasting. Deprivation of food, especially those that we've been addicted to, often leads to body aches and pains as well as bad moods and weariness. We are not called to trust our feelings but to persevere, even when we don't feel like it.

We don't know how Jesus "felt" during His 40-day fast, but we do know that He walked out of the wilderness in the power of the Holy Spirit. Don't gauge fasting success on feelings alone. God often rewards later in or after the fast rather than during the onset of the fast (there are exceptions, however). I had wonderful seasons of spiritual insight the last two weeks, but it was a difficult journey.

Week Three

My weight was 189 lbs. when the third week concluded. The first few days were tough. My toothache turned into a nightmare. Would I cave in and eat, take Amoxicillin, and get a root canal, or move forward with the fast? I wasn't being naive. Teeth are very similar to bones and can heal. Many people have reversed cavities through proper nutrition, but a root canal issue is different. The damage is deeper and more intense. I was curious to see what would happen.

I believe that antibiotics should be the last resort, not the first. The word *antibiotic* actually means "against life." Some antibiotics also affect DNA in very negative ways. They wipe out all bad bacteria as well as good bacteria, but they will not always fix the main cause of the infection. Many find themselves constantly battling chronic sickness and endless medications because the body is rarely fed what it needs to fight disease, and fasting is rarely used to reboot the system and promote healing.

During this third week I had water only, and I finally kicked the coffee habit right before the week began. I'm not making this an absolute rule for everyone. I'm simply sharing how quitting coffee greatly improved my life. If you can enjoy this freedom without it affecting you, that's wonderful, but you may want to research it. The effect on the body, including the heart, is something you should be aware of. *This is not what we "want" to hear, but it is what we "need" to hear.* My morning devotional life had been greatly affected for many years by coffee. I was seeking it before God, and it was difficult to concentrate and meditate on God's Word with my body in constant "fight or flight" mode.

By this time in the fast, I noticed that my sleep was deep, and I wasn't very hungry. I could have eaten, but the feeling wasn't strong. Remember, fasting is not starving. Hunger does not keep increasing every day as the fast continues. This is another myth that keeps countless people from fasting. During fasting your body switches its fuel source while it consumes diseased cells and tissue. Ghrelin, known as the hunger hormone, will signal your brain to eat, but it can be suppressed until true hunger resumes. The ghrelin signal to the brain has largely been conditioned to respond to our lifestyle; it's often not a true indication of genuine hunger.

Some say that you should stay busy; others say rest. I'm a promoter of rest, but if it's a matter of breaking the fast because you're bored, then stay busy. On the Sunday when this third week began, I arrived at five in the morning for early morning worship, followed by preaching at two services. Staying busy helped a great deal. I rarely exercised up to this point—healing and rest were key. My blood pressure was also in the target range. I kept reminding myself of fasting myths—that I wasn't going to die, lose all my muscle, or completely deplete myself of minerals and electrolytes.

Through my studies, I found that vitamins, minerals, and electrolytes are often stored in the body for seasons of fasting. God knew what He was doing. Granted, this is another good reason to have medical super-vision. If deficiencies are causing symptoms such as severe cramping, numbness, tingling in the fingers, irregular heart rhythms, and so on, those supervising might recommend supplementation. This was the case in 1973 when a 27-year-old man water fasted for 382 days under the supervision of the Scotland University. His weight dropped from 456 lbs. to 180 lbs.[32] *Ironically, those with many extra pounds are deficient, but those fasting rarely are.*

At one point in the fast, I heard that magnesium citrate can clear the intestinal tract, so I bought a bottle. Bad idea. I felt sick until I drank a cup of raw milk and ate a few nuts. Perfection would say, "You blew it. Start over." But that's not true. I wasn't about to let that sidetrack me, just as I wouldn't quit if I slipped and lost my footing in a race. Hardcore fasting advocates may not agree, but that's okay. They aren't in my shoes or yours. I have a responsibility to fulfill my obligations, and I need strength to do it. Once I consumed even that minimal amount, it sparked hunger; it was very

---

[32] The University of Scotland oversaw his fast for the entire period. Blood glucose levels held around 30 mg/100 ml consistently during the last eight months of the fast.

difficult not to eat. Had it not been for my toothache, I might have caved in further.

A quick word about cleansing the colon, either through enemas or other remedies—experts are divided; you may want to research this beforehand.

It's important to differentiate between the physical benefits and the spiritual benefits of fasting. The very light food intake mentioned earlier didn't affect my spiritual health, but giving the body light nourishment may slow down and hinder the healing process slightly. It also affects ketone levels (e.g., fat used as fuel). Catabolism is the breakdown of molecules to form simpler, healthier ones; energy is released, and healing occurs. Lengthy catabolism via fasting is what most bodies need for healing and regeneration, but food intake will slow it down.

One of the most difficult challenges for me was the extra time that I had. When I wasn't eating or preparing to eat or making something to eat or driving to get something to eat, I had extra hours each day. Instead of lunch and dinner with family and friends, I had to stay busy doing different things. It was hard, but not impossible. Hunger did subside, but altering my lifestyle was difficult because so much of it was tied to food.

One thing that differed from my seven-day fast a few months prior was that I was sleeping much better during this fast. During past fasts, growth hormone levels were probably elevated, along with adrenaline. I could not get to sleep before eleven o'clock at night. I'm not sure what changed this time; prior fasts may have played a role in stabilizing hormones.

If you find it difficult to sleep, be encouraged—it's part of the process. When I wake in the morning, I'm no longer dragging myself out of bed. I can get up easily and focus quickly. But remember, when you stop eating bad food there may be withdrawals in addition to fasting fatigue. It's part of cleansing. The first few days of the fast, I made sure that I had nothing on the calendar.

Throughout the last few weeks, anger would rise up from time to time, followed by great calm. Fasting not only cleanses the body but cleanses the emotions as well. Don't be surprised if your mood changes often. I also realized that I hadn't felt like taking a nap every afternoon over the last few weeks. Instead of feeling run down near lunchtime, I often felt like jogging. When you're not eating, your body doesn't waste energy on digestion.

If you can fight through the detox process and rest, that's the best option. Again, it's not about perfection but direction. Men, we must share the burden with our wives; allow them seasons of fasting while you help with the children and the chores. Marriage is a partnership.

During a fast, urine often becomes dark due to toxins being removed, and ketone bodies (fat) continues to burn, increasing each day until stabilizing. Measuring sticks that show how many ketones are being released into the urine are available at most drugstores. Urinalysis strips are also available that measure nitrite, pH, proteins, specific gravity, glucose, bilirubin, and leukocytes levels in addition to ketones. Numbers can be fun for health enthusiasts.

Breaking the fast

As I was driving home from church on the 22nd day, I felt tremendous peace about ending the fast. There was also a sense of accomplishment. I no longer had any motivation to fast. It was the first time in many years that I went this long without processed sugar, caffeine, and meat. The breakdown was as follows: *14 days of water out of 22 days; the last 9 were consecutive water days. My weight dropped from 204 lbs. to 189 lbs.*

Re-feeding the body was difficult. I ate some fruit and vegetables with organic hummus. I had to leave the kitchen and do something else for a few hours. I reintroduced more food over the next few days—papayas, oranges, strawberries, nuts, and many vegetables. However, I ate more than I should have, and my stomach paid the price.

On the first day after the fast, I waited until lunch to eat. This is a form of intermittent fasting. Even though the fast was over, this was a critical stage. Most people go right back into bondage after fasting, but you can be different. Allow the body to continue to heal through proper nutrition. It's been said that low valleys follow mountaintop experiences. This seemed true once I hit the third week. My four-year-old broke her leg and my oldest daughter popped her knee out of place. Two of my other children became sick, and my wife had to leave for Arizona for an emergency.

Don't be surprised if you experience valleys; they are part of the journey. This is when you are tested. Will you turn back to junk food, sugar, alcohol, nicotine, and so forth, or will you stay the course? *The flesh reminds you about the pleasure of indulging but not the consequences.* Once you cave in, depression and discouragement often follow. This is when you must get back on track regardless of how you feel. **Don't allow a temporary step back to become a long-term setback.**

Fasting conclusion

Through a series of fasts over the last two and a half years, my weight dropped from 240 lbs. to my lowest of 189 lbs. Again, it's important not to focus solely on weight.

My current *health plan* is outlined in the next chapter. The word *diet* can indicate short term, but a short-term solution cannot fix a long-term problem. That's why diets don't work. *Fasting and healthy lifestyle choices succeed when diets fail.* The miracle of fasting is that while it cleanses the body, it also cleanses the soul and strengthens us spiritually. My hope is that you too experience all the benefits of fasting.

My top five measurable spiritual changes while fasting:

1. Fasting fostered a deep and intimate prayer life. I could focus completely on God the first few hours of the day. Many prayers were answered during and after the fast.

2. Worship music touched my heart at a very deep level, more so than it normally did.

3. The Scriptures came alive, and my sermon preparation time benefited. Writing flowed abundantly when God brought things to mind.

4. My attitude and patience with others greatly improved. I could handle stress much easier. The phrase "roll with the punches" had new significance.

5. It was much easier to say no to temptation.

My top five measurable physical changes while fasting:

I'm not suggesting that everyone will experience these results or that old injuries and aches will not return, such as a toothache, poor vision, or joint pain. I'm merely outlining the benefits that I experienced while fasting. Many days were difficult; I simply had to press through.

1. My eyesight improved; the blurry vision faded. I no longer needed reading glasses. (I do use them when reading small font.)

2. My sleep was deep and extremely satisfying. I was well energized when I awoke. This felt strange after many years of feeling sluggish. I no longer had a strong desire for coffee or sugar in the morning, and I was able to wait until lunch to eat my first meal.

3. My hands rarely fell asleep during the night, and joint pain decreased substantially. My lower back pain decreased as well, and I became much more flexible.

4. My heart rate and blood pressure dropped. I was more relaxed, focused, and patient. My skin and complexion appeared healthier as well.

5. When I resumed exercising, I could run faster, farther, and longer.

I don't know what the future holds, but within the last few years, I have not been sick. In the past, I dealt with chronic sore throats, nasal congestion, coughing, and colds every few months. Fasting has proven to be very helpful in this area.

PART FIVE
My Lifestyle Plan

What Did My Blood Say about Healthy Choices?

Before releasing this book, I asked my doctor to order a blood panel. This was my opportunity to answer lingering questions. I wanted to see, on paper, what works and what doesn't.

In Leviticus 17:11, we read that "the life of the flesh is in the blood." The context involves temporarily covering sin until Christ's work on the cross. It's a beautiful story of redemption. But life, vitality, and health are also reflected in the blood. Blood supplies oxygen to tissues and cells and guards against infection. It also provides essential nutrients to vital areas and removes waste material.

Granted, it's impossible to get a perfect picture of what's going on, but a thorough blood panel can offer a panoramic view of what is taking place inside the body. The more your doctor can see, the better. For example, if I notice low blood platelet counts, I look at my diet. Am I getting enough vitamin B12 through meat and dairy? Those who avoid meat and dairy often struggle with low levels of B12. They may even have a low blood platelet count and a high MPV count. This often means that bone marrow is producing platelets at a rapid rate. Foods containing B12 can help offset this, as can supplementation.

In addition to vitamins, I also look at things such as glutathione, homocysteine, fatty acids, and hormones as well as cholesterol, HDL/LDL levels, triglycerides, and so on. **Our blood speaks volumes if we listen.** During the month leading up to this panel, I ate what many consider to be a "healthy" diet. For 30 days, I had a cup of coffee and a pastry for breakfast. I also ate vegetables and fruit as well as nuts. I didn't consume a lot of meat or dairy, but I did have so-called healthy chips and crackers each day.

As stated previously, most items labeled "healthy" aren't always healthy. Many companies use health-related words for marketing purposes such as *all-natural*, *heart-healthy*, and *gluten-free*. For this reason, it's important to read ingredient labels and nutrition facts listed on the back to see the full picture. The packaging might say "organic," but what are the ingredients? What is the sugar content? I recently purchased organic oat milk that had "heart-healthy" written on the front. The ingredients didn't list sugar, but the nutrition facts revealed a whopping 20 grams, or 5 teaspoons, of sugar in one cup—how is that "healthy" for the heart?

As another example, the popular ingredient carrageenan is a thickening agent derived from seaweed. Most nutritionists recommend avoiding products containing it. More information can be found in the article entitled "What is Carrageenan?" at WellnessMama.com.

I didn't fast during the 30-day period leading up to the first blood panel. Changes in my body were evident. I gained weight and became anxious and irritable. This diet was also affecting my heart, evidenced by shortness of breath. My workouts and energy suffered as well. Overall, I didn't feel good. To add insult to injury, many of the things that vanished during the long fast a month prior, such as blurred vision, joint pain, and lower back trouble, quickly returned.

To be honest, I didn't want to stop eating this way—sugar, coffee, and carbs once again became strongholds. But how were they affecting my blood? Did reintroducing a little coffee and sugar and refined oils really make a difference? Those were my burning questions, and I was about to find out the answers.

After the initial blood panel reading came in, I made healthy changes. Plants became my primary source of food—organic colorful salads and nuts and fruit. I also consumed a serving or two of organic meat and dairy each day and added a day of fasting.

I chose food in an unaltered state without chemicals and additives when possible and avoided stimulants like coffee, soft drinks, and energy drinks for two weeks before the second blood panel. I replaced harmful refined sugars with healthy honey or coconut sugar and reduced their intake to approximately six teaspoons a day. Obviously, it's nearly impossible to follow any plan perfectly. **The key is to make more right choices than wrong ones and to focus on health more than failure.**

This approach is nothing new. Many authors, such as Rex Russell, Jordan Rubin, and Joel Fuhrman have written extensively on it. Granted, Rubin and Russell promote higher dairy and meat consumption than I do, but their resources are very helpful. Ironically, the same publisher who published *The Maker's Diet* by Jordan Rubin approached me in 2001 to publish my first book, *What Works When "Diets" Don't*. When I declined their offer, they chose Rubin's book. God called me to be a pastor. Health is my passion, but preaching is my calling. *Feasting and Fasting* is an abridged version of my diet book, and it contains up-to-date information.

My top five blood panel results

After following my health plan for just two weeks, the results were as follows:

- **LDL-cholesterol** dropped from 123 mg. to 115 mg.

- **Total cholesterol** dropped from 192 to 178.

- **Triglycerides** dropped from 122 to 78.

- **Cholesterol ratio** dropped from 4.2 to a healthy ratio of 3.9.

- **Testosterone** rose from 346 to 569, and **free testosterone** went from 34.9 to 62.3. (Free testosterone is the testosterone that's available to affect anabolic activity such as muscle growth.) Both increases were encouraging.

Conclusion: Granted, the results could be considered anecdotal since I only monitored myself, but in as little as two weeks, my blood panel showed measurable positive results. Physically speaking, the added sugar, coffee, and refined oils had wreaked havoc on my body. I felt much better when I stopped consuming these products. My attitude improved, and I experienced more energy and deeper sleep.

My Personal Health Plan

Although my mother did a great job promoting health, once I left home my days were marked with alcohol abuse and junk food—a cinnamon roll and coffee was breakfast; fast food was dinner. Granted, I tried to eat healthy as often as I could, but it was a major challenge. At 19, I began using steroids such as Sustanon 250, which is a blend of four esterized testosterone compounds. I also took plenty of tablets—from Dianabol to Anavar to Anadrol. My past may someday catch up with me.

When I was younger, I didn't care about dying early if I could eat whatever I wanted to eat. I failed to realize that poor eating habits affect the quality of life—from depression and anxiety to poor health and chronic illness.

Most of us know what to do—we just have a hard time doing it. We need motivation and direction. For this reason, I simplified my personal plan by focusing on just a few key points. **If these six points become your priorities, you'll be well on your way to better health:**

1. *Is your spiritual health going in the right direction?* My hope is that readers don't become obsessed with fitness; real health has spiritual health at the center. Jeremiah 29:13 is a favorite verse of mine: "You will seek me and find me when you seek me with all your heart." We must first discipline ourselves before desire comes. We must first empty ourselves to be filled. We must first pray before there is transformation. And we must first seek Him if we are to truly find Him. It all begins with a choice. (More can be found at the sermon series on *Revelation* at WCFAV.org; try to listen to all seven messages.)

2. *Knock out the heavyweights early in the fight.* This is vitally important. Addiction to things such as caffeine, nicotine, unnecessary medications, sugar, alcohol, and toxic food should be eliminated as soon as possible. This first step in the right direction often leads to the next step. As I wrote earlier, avoid fake sweeteners such as aspartame, also known as AminoSweet, Nutrasweet, and Equal, at all costs. They are chemicals, not natural sweeteners.

3. *Less is more.* The less we eat, the better. Try to stop when satisfied rather than full, and rest the digestive tract as much as possible. Fortunately, nutrient-dense vegetables are low in calories and will satisfy the body. A large bowl of kale, brussels sprouts, asparagus, and a few nuts all mixed with homemade hummus is packed full of nutrients and may contain as little as 400 calories. As stated earlier, when I have sugar, I aim for 6 teaspoons, or 24 grams. That's one and a half pop-tarts for the whole day, or in my case, one large vegan cookie.

4. *Move more—a lot more.* When possible, center activities around activity rather than food. Big and bulky may be the look for Hollywood, but lean and less is healthier. Try to stay busy; it burns more energy, and it's biblical. Help people often, take long walks, visit people in nursing homes, volunteer more; the list is endless. Recall my early mention from Harvard Medical School: "Exercise keeps arteries healthy. . . . It also helps by improving other atherosclerotic risk factors such as high blood pressure, diabetes, obesity, stress, and various other factors that promote blood clots."[33] Exercise isn't just about working out, it involves moving like God designed us, and that often involves serving others. If you find that you have plenty of time for the gym but no time for others, your priorities need adjusting.

5. *Green feeds the machine, and colorful is powerful; meat and dairy are secondary.* As stated before, I lean toward a plant-based, whole foods approach because of the effect on the body, but I also add a little raw dairy or organic meat now and then. After all, Jesus no doubt ate fish

---

[33] "Exercise and your arteries" Harvard Health Publishing, Harvard Medical School, https://www.health.harvard.edu/newsletter_article/Exercise_and_your_ar teries.

and lamb, but most of the fish today, such as farmed salmon, is unhealthy due to farming practices and the presence of PCBs (dangerous man-made chemicals).

If I consume meat and dairy, my goal is around 10 percent. If I eat 2,500 calories a day, I shoot for 250 calories from meat or dairy (e.g., a cup of raw milk and a small chicken breast). Granted, I don't track this or pay attention to it; I simply eat it in moderation. When vegetables become the primary food, we naturally eat less meat. The biggest item on your plate should be a well-colored salad. Meat can be used for seasoning now and then. There's no harm in going a few days without animal products. Additionally, prepare food at home as often as possible since very few restaurants focus on health above profit.

I promote *primarily* plant-based food because it leads to cleaner arteries and a healthier digestive system. Studies have shown that blood samples of men who ate primarily plant-based foods for a year had many times the cancer-stopping power than those who didn't. But what if moderate meat-eaters also consumed the same number of disease-defeating phytochemicals in plants and incorporated a balanced diet, exercised, and lost weight? I believe they would be pleasantly surprised.

The high amount of water in plants also helps with hydration and energy. Hydration affects everything from heart health to joint movement to eyesight. Additionally, plant-based foods are rarely addictive. Most of us don't wake at midnight craving kale. Anything worth doing is often difficult, including healthy eating.

- *Finicky fats.* When eating good fats, avoid eating too many unless you're trying the ketogenic approach. When it comes to nuts, aim for raw and sprouted, but sometimes labels can be misleading. For example, cashews aren't raw unless you pick them from a cashew nut tree. Cashews sold in stores are pre-cooked, and almonds in California are pasteurized. But don't get obsessed with perfection. Enjoy good fat from nuts, avocados, flaxseed, coconuts and so on. *Remember, the life of the food gives life to the body.* We need good fats—from our brain that contains fats to all our cells that need fat to function (not to mention maintaining healthy skin)—fat is essential. That's why they are called *essential fatty acids.* Recall my earlier comment that I'm a proponent of eating the actual food. When possible, I use olives instead of olive oil, avocados instead of avocado oil, and almonds instead of almond oil. Not only is the breakdown of food slower, thus slowing fat storage, the uptake of nutrients and fiber is substantially higher when eating the whole product versus the oil.

6. *Consider intermittent fasting.* Intermittent fasting is not a fad; it aligns with how God designed us for seasons of feast and seasons of famine using fat as fuel during famine. Intermittent fasting provides a much-needed break from food, and it's a great way for the beginner to begin fasting. For example, if your last meal is early evening, then you wouldn't eat again until lunch the following day. This gives the digestive tract close to 16 hours of rest and may change insulin levels enough to affect health in a positive way. Remember, increased insulin and good health don't necessarily go together. Think of all the oxidative stress that you'll be avoiding with intermittent fasting when you miss breakfast consisting of unhealthy bacon and eggs or other harmful foods.

By fasting for at least 16 hours, stored sugar is burned, and the body may begin to use fat for fuel depending on how many carbohydrates have been stored. Most of your muscle is spared because the body switches to protein sparing during this time. Unless you have been limiting carbohydrates for a few days prior to the fast, ketosis (fat used as fuel) usually doesn't begin until hour 16. I fast this way, especially on weekends before preaching. I also try to fast for at least a week every 4 or 5 months. But if you're still consuming more calories than you're burning, they will be stored.

- *Ketogenic diets.* This approach may be beneficial now and then for those who aren't able to exercise or lose weight and for diabetics. Sometimes we need to jumpstart our system by rebooting it. Research healthy ketogenic approaches by Dr. Axe and other reputable sources.

My Daily Routine

This routine might sound like an obsession to some, but for the sake of this book, I detailed my example. However, I don't give it much thought anymore, and now it's a lifestyle with health in mind—not an obsession.

I begin the day around four o'clock in the morning with worship, prayer, and Bible reading, followed by walking, jogging, or bike riding. I try to exercise outside when possible; the gym environment is not ideal, and the intake of clean oxygen outside is often a better choice. Additionally, outside activity is a wonderful time to realign our heart with God.

When possible, I don't eat in the morning, but if I do, it's a small amount. Lunch consists of fruit and nuts or a plant-based shake consisting of organic almond milk, carob powder, banana, and protein mix, or a bowl of cooked veggies mixed with avocado and chicken. Dinner is along the same lines. I allow for an occasional sweet treat such as cacao with coconut sugar, and I have dessert with family and friends on certain occasions.

My 13-year-old daughter recently made chicken pot pie for dinner. I wasn't about to scrutinize the ingredient list. I sat down and enjoyed the meal with my family. My mom also drops off homemade cookies now and then. I try not to get too carried away. **We must be flexible when life calls for flexibility but firm when it calls for firmness.**

If I have organic meat, it's usually four ounces with a large salad. If I have raw dairy, it's either kefir with honey or raw milk in a shake now and then, or I mix raw milk with Ezekiel cereal and honey. I have organic eggs from time to time. Obviously, this may change in the future if my convictions change.

There are seasons when I avoid meat and dairy altogether. Find out what works for you and stick with it. For instance, ordering a blood test 30 days into a program can be compared to past lab results as a way of gauging success or for motivation to make changes. We must consider overall health rather than a toned physique. What's going on inside the body is more important than how the outside looks.

Years ago, I supervised many personal trainers. A large percentage of them looked great even though they ate fast food and abused their bodies with alcohol and steroids. *A perfect ten is not our goal but a healthy, God-*

honoring body is. As you move forward, don't allow a step back to become a setback. Very few people eat perfectly; however, they learn to make more right decisions than wrong ones. As a result, they eventually develop a healthier, more energetic lifestyle. It's truly that simple.

Hit the reset button often by fasting and by making health a lifestyle (not an obsession). The words *couch potato* are not in the Bible, but *lazy* and *slothful* are. We all struggle in this area, but don't let a struggle become a way of life. Turn off the internet, take a walk, and pray. This simple daily routine will lead to change.

Fuel motivation by reading articles and books and listening to sermons. Messages that I have given on health and fasting are listed at the end of this book. **The fact that we are destroying our bodies should be motivation enough.** Obesity among our youth is alarming—we are setting them up for failure before life even begins. View health as a journey with occasional setbacks. Many people, after slipping back into old patterns, act as if all their hard work was meaningless, and they quit. They allow a temporary problem to control their future, but you can be different. As they say in martial arts, "The only difference between a white belt and a black belt is that the black belt didn't give up." The only difference between those who succeed and those who fail is that those who succeed keep getting up—they fall forward!

You can start today; get back on track. Your body will change. There are people who crave broccoli dipped in hummus as well as avocados and tomatoes. You can too! **Don't let a step back become a setback!**

What Does It Profit You?

Again, at the end of the day, the most important aspect of health is spiritual health. Throughout my twenties, I continued to run from God, searching for identity and truth in everything but His Word. By age 28, I had climbed the corporate ladder. Money and success became my gods and ultimately controlled my life. I was driven, but for the wrong reasons. I felt a sense of purpose, but it often left me empty. I was passionate, but for the wrong things.

Strength to me was bench-pressing over 400 pounds, drinking beer, and winning fights. What I failed to realize was that I was weak. I was dying spiritually. I didn't have control of my life—my life had control of me. As a result of my misguided focus, my life took several unnecessary turns for the worse. By then, alcohol, anger, and arrogance had taken their toll. My life was crumbling around me.

Depressed and desperate for direction, I began to thumb through the pages of my Bible shelved long ago. Two Scriptures seemed to jump from the pages: "For what profit is it to a man if he gains the whole world, and is himself destroyed or lost?" (Luke 9:25) and "Today, if you will hear His voice: 'Do not harden your hearts, as in the rebellion'" (Ps. 95:8; see also v. 7).

I suddenly realized just how far I had drifted from the truth. I was at a turning point. I could choose to humble myself and turn to God or continue to reject Him. By God's grace, I put my complete trust in Him—joy, happiness, and peace filled my heart. During the months that followed, my passion and purpose for life became clearer than ever.

For those who doubt the existence of God, just look around. The fine-tuning of the universe is impossible without a Creator—from the perfect distance of the sun from the earth to the atmosphere's perfect balance to support life, we see that only a Designer could design such a complex system. How could the human body have evolved, broken off into different sexes, and produced children? It's impossible! The exact placement of the kidney, liver, heart, and lungs, along with the intricate design of the skeletal, muscular, and nervous systems, would be impossible without a Creator.

Anthony Flew (1923–2010) was once the world's most famous atheist, but in 2004 he shocked the world—he left atheism: "The integrated complexity of life itself—which is far more complex than the physical Universe—can only be explained in terms of an Intelligent Source."[34] He went on to say that Christianity is the most persuasive argument. In short,

---

[34] "Exclusive Flew Interview" (Anthony Flew's interview with Dr. Benjamin Wiker on October 30, 2007), ToTheSource, http://tothesource.org/uncategorized/exclusive-flew-interview/.

there must be a Creator. **Evolution is not a fact; it's a theory in crisis.** (For more information, search for "Put God to the Test" at WCFAV.org.)

Richard Dawkins, an evolutionary biologist at Oxford, made the following statement: "The fact that life evolved out of literally nothing, some 10 billion years after the universe evolved out of literally nothing, is a fact so staggering that I would be mad to attempt words to do it justice."[35] Yet that's exactly what we do when we try to explain away God.

Is your current belief system producing assurance, purpose, and peace, or is it bringing discouragement, disappointment, and despair? Turn to God; full surrender and repentance must take place. They are the keys to true fulfillment.

We hear a great deal about God's judgment and what can keep us from heaven, and rightly so, because "the fear of the Lord is the be-ginning of knowledge" (Prov. 1:7). But we also need to reflect on God's goodness, love, mercy, and grace. It's difficult to transmit my love for Jesus in this short book. He healed my brokenness and restored my life, and He can do the same for you. There is a deep longing inside all of us that cannot be satisfied until we recognize our need for a Savior and turn to Him. Romans 10:9 states that "if you confess with your mouth the Lord Jesus and believe in your heart that God has raised Him from the dead, you will be saved." (Check out John 3:1–21.)

I could write an entire book on my failures, but instead, I try to follow the apostle Paul's advice, and I encourage you to do the same: "Forgetting those things which are behind and reaching forward to those things which are ahead" (Phil. 3:13). If you truly grasp hold of this truth, it can motivate and encourage you beyond measure. Though the road ahead may be uncertain at times, the solid ground beneath will never shift. It's all about Whom you know.

---

[35] Richard Dawkins, *The Ancestor's Tale: A Pilgrimage to the Dawn of Evolution* (New York: Houghton Mifflin, 2004), 613.

Appendix 1:
Four Fasting Testimonies

"Fasting is difficult and grueling for the mind and body. However, both were refreshed, cleansed, and invigorated afterwards, and still are five days later. I had a lot of energy the next day, and I could think clearly. During the last eight days, I have experienced an incredible amount of healing taking place in my marriage. In retrospect, I did not realize how broken my marriage had become. I have never felt so close to God and been so in tune to His will for me in my life." – *Paula*

"I was fasting and seeking God a few years ago. I simply prayed at one point and asked God how I could get closer to Him. I immediately heard the answer back internally, as clearly as if someone was speaking to me, saying, "Stop taking drugs." I was so surprised. I answered back saying, "I don't take any drugs; what do you mean?" One word clearly came right back to me: *caffeine*. So I quickly went online and looked it up and was blown away about just how serious a drug it actually is, and how it can affect people so negatively, health-wise and in other areas ... thank you, WCF, for your ministry." – *Mike*

"I kept trying to fast, but I also kept failing. However, once I prayed for strength and made up my mind to finish, God pulled me through. It was one of the hardest things I've ever done in regard to health. But the power outweighed the pain. My relationship with God and my prayer life were reignited. Praise God! He is a Rewarder of those who seek Him with diligence and perseverance." – *Chris*

"Fasting has changed my life in an amazing way, and now I know exactly why it is so hard to do—it puts you in alignment with God and Satan hates it. I had a temper with my family—getting upset with the stupidest little things, yelling over nothing. My family was suffering from it. I knew I needed to change, and I heard caffeine played a huge role in mood swings. So I started fasting from soda and my attitude improved. Then I fasted from coffee and cut out caffeine. After that, God really calmed my spirit and helped me think about what came out of my mouth before I said anything. Then I decided to fast for two days on water only, but that turned into four days. God really convicted me on the way I treat my family. How can I go to church and portray a Christ-like life, but yell at my wife and kids and have them fear me while at home? So I cried out to God to change my heart and He did. I felt a massive shift of His peace and love take over, and my anger is totally controllable. I'm not going to say it's gone completely, but God changed my heart through fasting. . . . I'm so grateful for that." – *Jack*

Appendix 2:
Recommended Sermons

If you struggle with discipline and fasting, these sermons may help. The list goes from the newest to the oldest. The first message I gave on fasting, "Overcoming Addictions through Fasting," was in 2011. I was 45 pounds heavier than I am now, when this book is being written. "The Fasting Forum" message covers a great deal of what was outlined in this book. I highly recommend sharing it.

The Fasting Forum (full version): https://vimeo.com/260674192

Lean, Mean, Fasting, Machine: https://vimeo.com/253246415

The Pain of Discipline over the Pain of Regret: https://vimeo.com/252159286

Health—What Does the Bible Say?: https://vimeo.com/231641933

Fasting Over Forks pt. 1: https://vimeo.com/224003262

Fasting Over Forks pt. 2: https://vimeo.com/224932899

A Prisoner of Appetite: https://vimeo.com/197731085

The Hidden Treasure of Fasting: https://vimeo.com/101886639

Fasting—The Good, the Bad, and the Hungry: https://vimeo.com/172356334

Fasting—They Found the Secret: https://vimeo.com/172332319

This Does Not Go Out Except by Prayer and Fasting: https://vimeo.com/135808252

Fasting Breaks Enslavement: https://vimeo.com/57044810

Overcoming Addictions through Fasting: https://vimeo.com/25117942

Appendix 3:
Recommended Reading

Breaking the Stronghold of Food by Dr. Michael Brown is exceptional, and it's written from a Christian perspective. It doesn't focus on fasting per se but on other important elements of a healthy diet.

Fasting Can Save Your Life by Herbert M. Shelton is recognized as one of the all-time bestsellers on fasting. This book is a valuable resource even though it was written many years ago. Science has made many advances since its first publication, but the principles are timeless.

What the Bible Says about Healthy Living by Rex Russell and *The Maker's Diet* by Jordan Rubin are compelling resources for those wanting more information regarding what the Bible says about food. They grant more liberty with eating meat than what I promote.

God's Chosen Fast by Arthur Wallis is another exceptional resource that covers a lot more than what I can cover in this short book.

Fast Your Way to Health by J. Harold Smith outlines the physical and spiritual benefits of fasting. I appreciate his simple and straightforward approach.

The Power of Prayer and Fasting by Ronnie Floyd is an encouraging book for the pulpit as well as the pew. Although he is a pastor and talks about his 40-day juice fast experience, men and women from all walks of life can benefit from this resource, especially if you're hungry for revival.

A Hunger for God by John Piper is captivating and convicting. It focuses on desiring God more through fasting and prayer.

Fasting by Gordon Cove includes examples of people who fasted in the Bible and what the outcome was—encouraging, motivating, and convicting.

The Complete Guide to Fasting: Heal Your Body Through Intermittent, Alternate-Day, and Extended Fasting by Jimmy Moore and Dr. Jason Fung is not a biblical resource, but it is a good resource to truly understand how the body works, especially if you're struggling with diabetes, cancer, or heart disease. Although I don't agree with Dr. Fung's stance on evolution, eat the meat and throw out the bones (no pun intended for my plant-based diet friends). This book is lengthy and encourages heavy meat and fat consumption as well as the use of coffee. Although I understand where he's coming from regarding the ketogenic approach, I don't fully endorse it.

More Books from the Author

Desperate for More of God, the seventh book from Shane Idleman, focuses on the fully surrendered life. Do you want to mature in your faith? Are you ready to grow and change? This book can help.

Answers for a Confused Church seeks to clear the confusion surrounding controversial biblical topics.

One Nation 'Above' God serves as a wake-up call to Christian Americans that sitting on the sidelines is no longer an option for those who love their country and love their God. It makes a compelling case that almost all of America's current troubles are rooted in the growing abandonment of biblical principles.

What Works for Young Adults—Solid Choices in Unstable Times answers the top questions on the minds of young adults today such as: What is truth? How can I know God? Do all paths lead to heaven? What is God's will for my life? And many more. Group study questions included.

What Works for Men—Regaining Lost Ground is a challenging, biblically-based resource for men.

What Works for Singles—for Relationships, for Marriage, for Life is a motivational, biblically-based resource for those divorced, those marrying for the first time, and those currently single.

What Works When "Diets" Don't focuses on lifestyle changes rather than quick fixes.

More at http://shaneidleman.net/

21198026R00054

Made in the USA
San Bernardino, CA
02 January 2019